# CHOCOLATE!
# CHOCOLATE!

185 seductive recipes for
the uncontrollable chocoholic

## MARY NORWAK

CASSELL

FOR
JONATHAN, MATTHEW, ANDREW,
MICHAEL, HENRY, BERTIE AND JOSEPH
WHO ARE CURRENT AND FUTURE
CHOCOLATE-LOVERS

First published in 1993 by Cassell
This edition published 1997
Cassell
Wellington House, 125 Strand
London WC2R 0BB

Copyright © 1993 Mary Norwak
Designer: Richard Carr
Photographer: Laurie Evans

**British Library Cataloguing-in-Publication Data**
A catalogue record for this book is
available from the British Library

ISBN 0-304-34991-7

Typeset by Litho Link Ltd, Welshpool, Powys, Wales
Printed and bound in Spain by Graficromo S.A., Cordoba

# CONTENTS

1  ALL ABOUT CHOCOLATE ........................ 4

2  PRACTICAL MATTERS: ............... 7
Types of Chocolate and Chocolate Preparation

3  COMPLEMENTARY FLAVOURS ............. 13

4  CHOCOLATE CLASSICS ................ 16

5  HOT PUDDINGS ........................ 26

6  COLD PUDDINGS ....................... 36

7  ICES ........................................ 58

8  CAKES AND BISCUITS ................ 69

9  SWEETMEATS AND PETITS FOURS ..... 98

10  SAUCES .................................. 111

11  DRINKS ................................. 116

12  FANCY BITS ........................... 122

LIST OF RECIPES ....................... 125

INDEX .................................... 127

## Key to Recipes
☆ Easy
☆☆ Fairly easy
☆☆☆ Needs practice

# 1

# ALL ABOUT CHOCOLATE

..........................................

WHAT IS THIS CHOCOLATE PASSION, this consuming desire for a simple food which makes strong men weak, and sensible women useless? Why do civilised human beings crave chocolate and risk their money and their weight for sensuous gratification?

Perhaps the answer is that chocolate is not as simple as we think. It is a complex mixture of flavours and textures which provides comfort and nourishment, energy and satisfaction, and that magical quality which lifts the spirit. We eat it for pleasure, tinged with a naughty guilt. We feel wicked as we crunch and munch and wrap our tongues round creamy fillings. We pamper ourselves with the sheer luxury of chocolate, reward our efforts with its comfort, and share its pleasure with our loving friends. Chocolate is handy and accessible, quick and easy to eat, and horribly addictive.

Nobody need feel alone with a chocolate addiction, for sales of chocolate continue to rise. In 1996, over £3.5 billion was spent on it, supporting an enormous industry employing about 65,000 people who produce the stuff we love. Confectionery is the single largest packaged food market, above milk, bread, tea and coffee, and every Briton gets through an average of 20lb (9.4kg) of the stuff each year.

Chocolate has come a long way since its beginnings in Central and South America. The Aztecs and Mayans used the cacao bean for a drink consumed at such ceremonial functions as weddings and funerals, and the beans were offered to the gods. In Central America the beans were used as currency, and it was probably here that Columbus discovered them and took them back to Spain where nobody showed interest. Cortés landed in Mexico in 1519, was welcomed by Montezuma the great ruler, and first encountered the royal drink of chocolate or *xocoatl*.

The drink was bitter, but highly spiced and very frothy, and much prized for its energy-giving qualities. Cortés slaughtered the Emperor and destroyed his civilisation, but his soldiers took Mexican seeds of the cocoa trees on their subsequent journey. They planted cocoa trees in Africa on their way home, setting up an industry dominated by the Spaniards as chocolate was slowly introduced to Europe. The Spaniards sweetened their chocolate drinks with sugar and flavoured them with vanilla, bringing chocolate a little nearer to today's luxury.

When the drink first came to Britain, it was introduced through the chocolate house where men gathered in London's Bishopsgate in 1657. For many years chocolate was known only as a drink, made exactly as it had been in earlier times. Lumps of chocolate were broken and soaked in a little warm water until soft. More water was added and the mixture simmered for two hours, then was left to get completely cold. Fat settled on the top, which was taken off and discarded. The residual chocolate was then warmed with milk for the final drink, and it was recommended that it should be well beaten when warming so that the drink would thicken. Throughout the eighteenth and nineteenth centuries, doctors recommended chocolate as a restorative for energy and also as a soothing balm for the nerves. At the French court Madame du Barry served cups of reviving chocolate to her suitors, and it is said that Casanova preferred it to champagne.

Perhaps, surprisingly, chocolate took years to develop from a popular drink. In 1728, the first English factory was opened for processing the cocoa bean, but the first solid eating chocolate was not produced until 1847 by Messrs Fry & Sons. Development came more swiftly as the Dutch, Swiss and British worked on new ideas. The earlier and awkward chocolate 'nibs' were converted into simple cocoa liquids and powders; milk chocolate was introduced by the Swiss in 1875, who a few years later perfected the art of making very smooth eating chocolate. By 1900 chocolate was beginning to replace the earlier favourites such as toffee, formerly made in cottage kitchens. Milton Hershey developed his chocolate interests in America, saying 'chocolate is a permanent thing'. His prescience resulted in an American boom in the new confectionery, and today chocoholics gather in Hershey, Pennsylvania, for an annual chocolate festival of five days' indulgence and chocolate bingeing. In France, Switzerland and Britain new confectionery lines were developed after Jules Séchaud produced the first filled chocolate.

Curiously, nobody thought of chocolate or cocoa as a culinary ingredient. It is useless to search in nineteenth-century cookery books for recipes, because chocolate puddings and cakes simply did not exist. The confectioners and *pâtissiers* of middle Europe were the first to develop the luscious chocolate gâteaux and mousses we know today, to serve in their coffee houses with lashings of whipped cream. The taste for chocolate was given another boost as chefs began to finish meals with chocolate delicacies, later taken up by private cooks as the basic ingredients of plain chocolate and cocoa were promoted by manufacturers. Now chocolate is everywhere, easily purchased and easily used, and we may all share the sinful indulgence of the Austrian coffee house.

Chocolate is deliciously indescribable, a mouthwatering experience with a dark, melting, velvety richness. It is for the sybarite who has no wish for Puritan restraint, for the hedonist who doesn't care, for the gourmand with an all-consuming passion.

This book is not for the faint-hearted. It is for the enthusiast who cannot imagine life without chocolate. It is for the cook who always produces something chocolatey among her dinner-party puddings; for the comfort-lover who will order hot chocolate rather than coffee for that mid-morning pick-you-up; for the grown-up schoolboy who always chooses the chocolate cake; for the professed savoury-tooth who can never resist a piece of chocolate cake.

The recipes are the ultimate of their kind – the gooiest cake, the most syrupy sauce, the most sensational fudge, the almost unbelievable roulade and the deepest, fluffiest chocolate soufflé. While the recipes are seductive, they are mostly very simple to achieve. As a chocoholic, one knows that no true believer can spend hours on a complicated recipe because the most important ingredient will be eaten before it reaches the mixing bowl.

# 2

# PRACTICAL MATTERS:

## Types of Chocolate and Chocolate Preparation

················

WHEN PREPARING RECIPES it is important to use the best possible chocolate. If the raw material is of high quality, the resulting dish will be very special. Inferior ingredients produce inferior dishes.

There are many different types of chocolate which may be used, made from cocoa butter, chocolate liquor and sugar, and sometimes milk solids. Their value in cooking depends on the proportion of these essential constituents. In order to be called chocolate, not cake covering, the product must have a minimum of 30 per cent cocoa solids. Some chocolate contains as much as 70 per cent cocoa solids, and this may be checked by reading the packet information. European chocolate tends to be slightly more bitter than British, usually with a more brittle texture. Inevitably, good chocolate is expensive, but well worth spending money on for its depth of flavour, and the cost is usually offset by the relative cheapness of the other ingredients in a chocolate recipe.

## Types of Chocolate

### PLAIN CHOCOLATE

Made from cocoa butter, chocolate liquor, vegetable fats and sugar, with a good strong flavour and dark colour. Maybe labelled bitter, fondant or dessert. For everyday use, that with 30–40% cocoa solids is fine; with 70% cocoa solids, it is best for very special dishes and decoration.

### BAKER'S CHOCOLATE

Rarely found, this chocolate is totally unsweetened and sugar in a recipe must be adjusted to taste.

## MILK CHOCOLATE

Milk chocolate contains cocoa butter, chocolate liquor, vegetable fats and sugar, with milk solids replacing some of the chocolate liquor. It is paler in colour than plain chocolate and has less chocolate flavour, so it is rarely used in recipes.

## WHITE CHOCOLATE

Made from cocoa butter, milk and sugar, white chocolate is without colour as it contains no chocolate liquor. It is very sweet with only a light chocolate flavour, and is not easy to melt successfully. It is used in one or two recipes to give contrasting colour, but the flavour is so minimal that it is scarcely worth using.

## COUVERTURE

This chocolate for the professional cook contains a very high proportion of cocoa butter. It has a rich flavour, a high sheen and a brittle texture. It has to be tempered by repeated heating and cooling so that it melts successfully, and it is widely used by confectioners.

## CHOCOLATE CHIPS

Small dots of plain or milk chocolate are useful as they melt quickly, and they may be used without melting to provide the chocolate accent in biscuits, cakes and ice creams.

## CAKE COVERING

Often described as 'cooking chocolate', these are made with less than the required minimum of cocoa solids and do not qualify as chocolate. They contain added vegetable and/or coconut oil and do not have a strong flavour. They are, however, cheaper than pure chocolate, melt very easily and are easy to handle. The chocolate purist will shun a chocolate substitute, but cake covering may be used if cost is more important than flavour.

## COCOA POWDER

Unsweetened cocoa powder gives a strong flavour and is useful for baking. The flavour is released by adding a little very hot liquid to the cocoa powder before it is added to a recipe. European cocoa powder has a subtly different flavour, but may be used in the same way.

*Types of chocolate and decorations*

## DRINKING CHOCOLATE POWDER

This has a subtle chocolate flavour, but it is very sweet, pale and milky and is used only occasionally in baking when other ingredients can be adjusted accordingly.

# Chocolate Preparation

Chocolate is not difficult to use, but attention to detail is important as problems can occur which may make dishes unsightly. Particular care is needed in heating and setting chocolate.

## STORAGE

Chocolate should be stored in a cool, dry place, and plain chocolate will store well for a year without loss of colour or flavour (milk chocolate is best used within six months). Chocolate may be stored in a refrigerator or freezer but should be well-wrapped as it tends to pick up other flavours. It may acquire a greyish-white film or bloom because cocoa butter or sugar crystals may rise to the surface after exposure to differing temperatures or excessive moisture. This does not affect the flavour and will disappear after melting.

## CHOPPING AND GRATING

To speed melting, or to provide small pieces for recipes, chocolate may be chopped or grated. Chocolate may be chopped with a sharp knife or broken up in a food processor. A vegetable peeler or a grater may be used for grating. Be sure that the chocolate is firm and at room temperature before being prepared or it may melt in the hands and be difficult to handle.

## MELTING

Chocolate is very sensitive to heat and must be melted with great care. If melted on its own, it must be kept completely dry and no hotter than 110°F/44°C. Chocolate should not be melted on its own over direct heat or it will stiffen up and then cannot be reconstituted. There are three ways of melting chocolate successfully.

*1.* Break the chocolate into small pieces and put them into a bowl or top of a double saucepan. Bring a pan of water to the boil and put the bowl or top saucepan in place, so that the hot water does not touch the bottom of the upper container. Remove from the source of heat so that steam or water does not splash into the chocolate, which will make it seize up and discolour. Stir the chocolate as it melts so that it becomes very smooth. If necessary, reheat the water and replace the bowl or top pan to finish the melting process.

2. Break the chocolate into small pieces and warm in a very low oven (such as the warming oven of a range). The temperature should be no more than 225°F/110°C/Gas ¼.

3. Break the chocolate into small pieces and put into a microwave-proof bowl. Heat for 1–2 minutes in a microwave oven, checking with the manufacturer's instructions if possible. The chocolate will retain its shape but will become soft and smooth when stirred. Remember that foods retain heat and continue warming through after being microwaved, so be careful not to overheat the chocolate.

Do not cover a bowl in which chocolate is being heated, or condensation will form droplets of moisture which will fall back into the chocolate and ruin it.

Liquid may be mixed with chocolate before melting, so that the ingredients are heated together. 1–2 tablespoonsful of water, strong coffee or a spirit such as rum or brandy may be added in this way. If fat is to be added, butter or oil may be stirred in when the chocolate has melted.

## TEMPERING

This is a method of melting chocolate used by professional confectioners to give a perfect finish to their work. The chocolate used has a high proportion of cocoa butter and is repeatedly heated and cooled so that it finally melts and sets perfectly. This is not necessary with the eating chocolate generally used which has a lower proportion of cocoa butter.

## SETTING

Chocolate sets best at a fairly cool temperature of 65°F/18°C, but will set at a room temperature of about 72°F/22°C. At this higher temperature, setting will take a little longer, but the chocolate will retain its shape and shine. Do not try to set chocolate in a refrigerator as it develops a white bloom; choose a reasonably cool, dry place instead.

## DIPPING

If using chocolate to coat sweets or fruit, be sure to melt it in a wide bowl for easy use. Cool the chocolate to 92–110°F/33–44°C so that it is still liquid but will adhere to the object being dipped. For a smooth, shiny finish, add 1 tablespoon vegetable oil to 6oz (175g) chocolate.

Use a cocktail stick, skewer, fondue fork or confectionery fork to dip the items concerned; allow excess chocolate to drip off, and push off the dipped object with another skewer or cocktail stick. If items are placed on foil or baking parchment, they can be easily removed.

## MOULDING

Chocolate may be moulded in plastic, metal or paper moulds. They should be completely dry and clean so that the chocolate will not stick and crack. Polish plastic or metal moulds with a piece of kitchen paper so that the chocolate remains very shiny, and do not handle finished chocolates with the fingers as they mark quickly.

## SUBSTITUTION OF CHOCOLATE

If a small quantity of chocolate is needed for a recipe and is not available, it is possible to substitute 3 tablespoons cocoa powder, ½oz (15g) butter and 1 tablespoon sugar for each 1oz (25g) chocolate.

## MAKING MISTAKES

When chocolate is overheated, or when cold liquid such as water or cream is added to hot chocolate, it will 'seize' and become cloudy, dull and lumpy. It will usually have to be discarded, but it may be possible to rectify the situation by stirring in a little vegetable oil.

# 3

# COMPLEMENTARY FLAVOURS

...........................................

THERE IS A GREAT ART in improving and enhancing a dish by complementary flavouring. Cookery experts like to keep their flavouring secrets closely guarded, because knowing 'what goes with what' lifts their cooking out of the common rut. Complementary flavourings are meant to accent a dish and give it greater depth and complexity without smothering its basic flavour. Skilful use of these flavourings improves dishes beyond all recognition, and the cook's palate needs to be finely tuned to get the combinations right and to avoid the bad restaurant disaster of hare-and-apricots-wrapped-in-spinach-in-redcurrant-sauce-served-with-a-chocolate-biscuit type. Quantities of complementary flavourings are difficult to prescribe; successful results can only be gauged by the fineness of the creator's palate, and by the people who eat the finished dish.

Chocolate is a magnificent basic ingredient, strongly flavoured and stamping its own character on any dish which includes it. Even so, a chocolate recipe can be flat, dull and cloying without a hint of liqueur, a touch of spice or a surprise of fruit. The following list gives guidance on those flavourings which are the finest complements to chocolate.

## NUTS

The soft melting smoothness of chocolate is greatly enhanced by the crunch of nuts, particularly *walnuts*, *hazelnuts*, *almonds*, *pecans*, *Brazils* and *coconut*. An extra dimension is given when the nuts are lightly toasted or caramelised.

## CARAMEL

The slightly burnt sugar flavouring of caramel is a fine foil for chocolate, probably at its best when nut praline is used in recipes.

## DRIED FRUIT

The softness of dried fruit blends with chocolate and adds a light sweetness. Use *raisins*, *sultanas*, *candied peel* or *glacé fruit*. The texture and flavour are improved if the fruits are soaked in a little spirit, such as rum or brandy, before using in a recipe.

## SPIRITS AND LIQUEURS

A few drops of liqueur lift a chocolate mousse, a cake filling or a sauce to a different plane. There is no need to drown a dish in alcohol, and this is particularly important when a dish is not heated to remove the alcoholic effect. *Rum, brandy* and *whisky* accent chocolate and add a light flavouring of their own. More distinctive flavouring is given by liqueurs based on *coffee, chocolate, mint, orange, raspberry, blackcurrant* and *cherry*.

## HERBS AND SPICES

The combination of spice and chocolate is an old one, perhaps because they come from the same hot climate. The classics which enhance chocolate are *cinnamon, ginger* and *vanilla*. In a cooler climate, *peppermint* is a traditional accompaniment, giving a teasing sparkle to the heaviness of very dark chocolate. When using this flavouring, choose peppermint oil, rather than essence, which has a flat, synthetic flavour.

## FRUIT

The paradoxical sharp sweetness of fruit goes wonderfully with chocolate. Fresh fruit may be used in many dishes, while fruit jams make the perfect foil to chocolate cake. Use *pears, oranges, raspberries, strawberries, blackcurrants, apricots, cherries* and *pineapple*. For tremendous sophistication, try *cranberries*.

## COFFEE

Coffee and chocolate have an extraordinary relationship, and one which is as ancient and traditional as that of spice and chocolate, probably for the same reason that the two ingredients came from similar climates and areas of the world. The combination is usually known as *mocha*, and it will be found that a hint of coffee enhances a chocolate dish, just as a little chocolate gives depth to a coffee recipe. The flavouring may be introduced by using coffee liqueur, very strong black coffee, coffee essence or coffee powder.

# Chocolate and Wine

Chocolate provides real problems for the wine-lover, and it is notoriously difficult to partner with wine at the end of a meal. One solution for the strong-hearted is to offer a small glass of *Armagnac* or *rum* which will complement the dish. Those who dislike spirits will have a greater problem in coping with the sweetness of the chocolate and its mouth-coating texture. A compromise may be a fortified wine such as *Málaga* or *port*, which contain a stiffening of brandy.

Traditional champagne and the sweet muscat dessert wines are not good partners for chocolate. General consensus seems to be in favour of simple but characterful wines, which need to be good ones to stand up to the chocolate. A good *Sauternes* or *asti spumante* seems to work well, and so surprisingly do some dry red wines. It is a good idea to experiment before offering a wine and chocolate combination, and if in doubt, leave the idea alone. Serve the cheese course with its appropriate wine before the pudding, and then serve the chocolate dish and follow up with a good cup of coffee.

# 4

# CHOCOLATE CLASSICS

................................

*A few chocolate recipes have achieved the status of classic dishes. Mostly of French and Austrian origin, they are triumphs of the pâtissier's art, which look delectable and often complicated, and which are fine examples of the skills of combining flavours and textures to produce a perfect and altogether elegant result.*

*Nobody need be frightened of trying to reproduce these classic dishes. All pâtisserie consists of a number of relatively simple recipes combined in a unique way. If a cook can make a reasonable sponge cake, meringue, short-bread, butter icing, fruit glaze and caramel, the delicious recipes in this chapter may be easily achieved. The essential ingredient is time to make each component part as perfect as possible.*

## CHOCOLATE MARQUISE

☆☆

*This is a very light mousse but the flavour is intense and rich, since both chocolate and cocoa powder are used. Every chef has a personal recipe for Marquise, usually a closely-guarded secret.*

### INGREDIENTS

FOR 6–8

7 oz (200g) plain chocolate

3½oz (90g) unsalted butter

3 oz (75g) caster sugar

I oz (25g) cocoa powder

3 egg yolks

2 tbs rum or brandy

½ pt (300ml) double cream

Line a 1lb (450g) loaf tin with foil, smoothing down the creases carefully.

Break the chocolate into small pieces and put into a bowl over a pan of hot water. When the chocolate has melted, remove from heat and leave to cool. Whip the butter and half the sugar until very pale and creamy and work in the cocoa powder. Whisk the egg yolks and remaining sugar until almost white and very fluffy, and then whisk in the rum or brandy. Whip the cream to soft peaks.

Add the chocolate to the butter mixture and mix well. Gradually work in the egg mixture and finally fold in the cream. Pour into the prepared tin and chill for 4 hours. Turn out on to a serving dish. Serve in slices with any of the sauces on pp111–15.

# MARJOLAINE

☆☆☆

*A truly wonderful cake made from layers of nutty sponge with chocolate cream, coffee cream and praline cream, finished with more praline. The assembly is a little complicated but each stage of the preparation is easy, so that the cook only needs time to be successful.*

## INGREDIENTS

FOR ONE 9×6IN (22.5×15CM) CAKE

8 oz (225g) almonds
4 oz (100g) hazelnuts
8 oz (225g) caster sugar
1 tbs plain flour
1 tbs cocoa powder
8 egg whites

### filling

8 oz (225g) sugar
¼ pt (150ml) water
8 oz (225g) unsalted butter
3 tbs brandy
3 egg yolks
2 oz (50g) plain chocolate
1 tbs strong black coffee

### praline

8 oz (225g) almonds
4 oz (100g) sugar
2 tbs water

Preheat the oven to 400°F/200°C/Gas 6. Butter and flour two 12×9in (30×22.5cm) Swiss-roll tins. Dip the almonds into boiling water and slip off their skins. Grill the hazelnuts and rub off the skins. Mix the almonds and hazelnuts and grill until golden brown. Grind in a blender until fine and stir with 7oz (200g) sugar, the flour and cocoa powder until evenly coloured.

Whisk the egg whites to stiff peaks and gradually beat in the remaining sugar. Fold in the nut mixture. Spread over Swiss-roll tins and bake for 15 minutes. Cool in the tins for 5 minutes and then cool on a wire rack. Cut each cake in half.

To prepare the filling, put the sugar and water into a pan and boil to 240°F/116°C, when a little of the mixture dropped into cold water forms a soft ball. Take off the heat and cool to lukewarm. Beat the butter until very soft and light and gradually beat in the syrup, brandy and egg yolks. Divide the mixture in half and divide one half into half again. Melt the chocolate in a bowl over hot water and beat into one of the smaller portions. Flavour the other small portion with the coffee.

Prepare the praline by blanching the almonds in hot water and then grilling them until golden brown. Put the sugar and water into a heavy-based pan and simmer until it just begins to colour. Stir in the nuts until well coated and when the syrup is caramel colour, pour on to an oiled plate or marble slab. When cold, break into pieces and grind in a blender or food processor.

Fold half the praline into the large portion of filling. Put one cake on to a serving plate and spread with chocolate filling. Top with a second cake and spread with coffee filling. Top with the third cake and spread with half the praline filling. Top with the final cake and spread with remaining filling. Sprinkle with the remaining praline. Chill for 30 minutes before serving.

Overleaf: *Dobos Torte*

# DOBOS TORTE

☆☆☆

*This marvellous cake consists of thin layers of sponge sandwiched with chocolate cream, with the surface covered with a thick layer of caramel. It is a triumph of the Hungarian kitchen and used to be a speciality of Floris in Soho. It was always chosen for birthday celebrations by the staff of* Vogue *magazine.*

## INGREDIENTS

FOR AN 8IN (20CM) CAKE

8 oz (225g) unsalted butter

8 oz (225g) caster sugar

4 eggs

6 oz (175g) self-raising flour

½ tsp baking powder

pinch of salt

### filling

6 oz (175g) sugar

5 tbs water

2 egg yolks

6 oz (175g) unsalted butter

4 oz (100g) plain chocolate

### caramel

3 oz (75g) sugar

3 tbs water

Preheat the oven to 400°F/200°C/Gas 6. Grease three 8in (20cm) sandwich tins and dust lightly with flour. Beat the butter and sugar together until very light and creamy. Separate the eggs and beat in the yolks one at a time. Sieve together the flour, baking powder and salt and fold into the mixture. Whisk the egg whites to stiff peaks and fold into the mixture.

Using half the mixture, spread thin layers in each sandwich tin and bake for 8 minutes until golden brown. Allow to cool in the tins for 2 minutes and turn on to wire racks to cool. Re-grease and flour the tins and bake the remaining mixture to make six layers in all.

To make the filling, put the sugar and water into a heavy-based pan and heat gently until the sugar has dissolved. Bring to the boil and boil to 215°F/102°C, until the syrup spins a short fine thread from a spoon. Whisk the egg yolks in a bowl until thick and creamy and gradually beat in the hot syrup until the mixture is cool and fluffy. In a separate bowl, beat the butter until soft and light and add the egg mixture a little at a time, beating until smooth and shiny. Melt the chocolate in a bowl over hot water and beat into the mixture. Refrigerate while preparing the caramel.

To make the caramel, put the sugar and water into a heavy-based pan and stir over low heat until the sugar has dissolved. Bring to the boil and boil to 345°F/174°C, when the syrup will be clear and caramel-coloured. Spread this caramel evenly over the top of one cake layer, using an oiled knife. While still soft, mark into eight triangles with a sharp knife and leave to set.

Assemble the cake layers and chocolate cream on a serving dish, making each cream layer the same depth as each cake layer. Top with the caramel-covered layer and pipe any spare chocolate cream in whorls round the edge.

❖

### Cook's tip for making buttercream

*As soon as the syrup has reached the required temperature, remove from the heat. It is best to use an electric beater so that the syrup can be poured on to the eggs while beating continues. The egg yolks must be thick and creamy and the syrup must be added in a thin trickle. The butter should be at room temperature so that it can be beaten to a soft light creaminess.*

## BÛCHE DE NOËL

☆☆☆

*This chocolate Swiss roll with a rich chocolate filling and icing is the traditional French Christmas cake. The centre can also be filled with chestnut purée mixed with whipped cream and flavoured with orange liqueur for something extra special.*

### INGREDIENTS

FOR ONE LOG CAKE

4 eggs

4 oz (100g) caster sugar

3 oz (75g) self-raising flour

1 oz (25g) cocoa powder

### filling and icing

3 oz (75g) sugar

5 tbs water

4 egg yolks

6 oz (175g) unsalted butter

3 oz (75g) plain chocolate

2 tbs rum

a little icing sugar

Preheat the oven to 400°F/200°C/Gas 6. Grease and base-line a 12×9in (30×22.5cm) Swiss-roll tin. Whisk the eggs and sugar together until pale, thick and creamy. Sieve together the flour and cocoa powder and fold into the egg mixture. Spread in the prepared tin and bake for 12 minutes. Turn out on to a piece of greaseproof paper sprinkled with caster sugar. Peel off the lining paper. Trim the edges of the cake and roll up firmly with the paper inside. Cover with a clean tea cloth and leave until cold.

To make the filling, put the sugar and water into a heavy-based pan and heat gently until the sugar has dissolved. Bring to the boil and boil to 215°F/102°C, until the syrup spins a short fine thread from a spoon (see Cook's Tip, p.19). Whisk the egg yolks in a bowl until thick and creamy and gradually beat in the hot syrup until the mixture is cool and fluffy. In a separate bowl, beat the butter until soft and light and add the egg mixture a little at a time, beating until smooth and shiny. Melt the chocolate in a bowl over hot water and beat into the mixture with the rum.

Unroll the cake and spread with one-third of the filling mixture. Roll up and place on a serving dish or board. Cover with the remaining mixture and mark with a fork to look like a log. Chill for 1 hour. Just before serving, sprinkle with a little icing sugar to look like snow and decorate with robins and holly.

## DEVIL'S FOOD

☆☆☆

*An American favourite which combines a dense, dark chocolate cake with a white fluffy frosting. There is also Angel Food, which by contrast is a pure white cake.*

### INGREDIENTS

FOR AN 8IN (20CM) CAKE

8 oz (225g) light soft brown sugar

2 oz (50g) cocoa powder

¼ pt (150ml) milk

4 oz (100g) unsalted butter

2 eggs

8 oz (225g) plain flour

1 teasp bicarbonate of soda

### icing

1 lb (450g) sugar

¼ pt (150ml) water

2 egg whites

Preheat the oven to 325°F/160°C/Gas 3. Grease and line an 8in (20cm) round cake tin. Put the sugar, cocoa powder and milk into a pan with the butter. Heat gently until the butter and sugar have melted and the mixture is smooth. Leave until just cold. Beat in the eggs. Sieve the flour and bicarbonate of soda and beat into the mixture. Pour Into the tin and bake for 1 hour. Cool in the tin for 5 minutes and turn on to a wire rack to cool. When cold, split into three layers.

To make the icing, put the sugar and water into a heavy-based pan and stir over low heat until the sugar has dissolved. Boil to 240°F/116°C, when a little of the mixture dropped into cold water forms a soft ball. Whisk the egg whites to stiff peaks. Pour in the hot syrup gradually, whisking all the time, and continue whisking until the icing is thick and stands in soft peaks. Sandwich together the cake layers with this mixture and spread the remaining icing all over the cake. Leave to stand for 30 minutes before serving.

❖

### Cook's tip for making icing

*When making the icing, remove the syrup from the heat as soon as the correct temperature is reached. Add the syrup to the egg whites in a thin trickle, whisking all the time. Use the icing as soon as the mixture is thick and softly peaked.*

# CASSATA
## ☆☆

*This Sicilian confection is a fluffy combination of cheese with fruit peel and chocolate, wrapped in sponge cake and finished with chocolate – not the often debased version, which is just a mixture of ice cream and candied peel.*

### INGREDIENTS
FOR 8
1 lb (450g) curd cheese
2 oz (50g) caster sugar
4 tbs orange liqueur
4 oz (100g) chopped mixed candied peel
2 oz (50g) plain chocolate
8 trifle sponges

icing
6 oz (175g) plain chocolate
3 tbs strong black coffee
3 oz (75g) unsalted butter

Line a 2pt (1.2l) pudding basin with foil, press and smooth down the creases carefully.

Cream the cheese and sugar together until light and fluffy and work in half the liqueur. Add the peel. Chop the chocolate finely and fold into the mixture.

Split the trifle sponges in half and sprinkle the cut sides with the remaining liqueur. Line the base and sides of the basin with the sponge, cut-sides inwards, reserving a few pieces for the top. Fill with the cheese mixture and cover with remaining sponge. Cover and chill for 12 hours. Turn on to a serving dish.

To make the icing, put the chocolate and coffee into a bowl over a pan of hot water and heat gently until the chocolate has melted. Remove from heat and beat in small pieces of butter. Cool and spread over the pudding. Chill for 1 hour before serving.

## SACHER TORTE

☆☆☆

*The pride of Vienna, this rich, light chocolate sponge
is glazed with apricot jam before being finished with
a smooth chocolate glaze. It is often served with
a mountain of whipped cream.*

### INGREDIENTS

FOR A 9IN (22.5CM) CAKE

8 oz (225g) plain chocolate

1 tbs rum

8 oz (225g) unsalted butter

8 oz (225g) caster sugar

5 eggs

6 oz (175g) self-raising flour

### filling and icing

4 tbs apricot jam

4 oz (100g) plain chocolate

4 oz (100g) caster sugar

3 tbs water

2 drops olive oil

Grease and line a 9in (22.5cm) round tin. Preheat the oven to 300°F/150°C/Gas 2. Melt the chocolate with the rum in a bowl over hot water and leave to cool. Cream the butter and sugar until light and fluffy. Separate the eggs and beat in the yolks one at a time, then the melted chocolate. Sieve the flour and fold into the mixture. Whisk the egg whites to stiff peaks and fold into the chocolate mixture. Put into prepared tin and bake for 1½ hours. Leave in the tin for 15 minutes and turn on to a wire rack to cool. When cold, split into two layers. Sieve the jam and warm it slightly. With half the jam sandwich the layers together and brush the rest all over the cake.

To make the icing, melt the chocolate in a pan over hot water and leave until cool. Put the water and sugar into a heavy-based pan and simmer until the syrup is straw-coloured. Cool to lukewarm and stir into the chocolate. Add the oil and beat well. Smooth all over the cake. Leave to set for 1 hour.

## BLACK FOREST GÂTEAU

☆☆☆

*A tempting mixture of chocolate sponge, slightly
sharp cherries, kirsch, cream and plain chocolate –
very different from some of the versions served in a
cheap restaurant meal. It is not difficult to make,
but needs a little time and care.*

### INGREDIENTS

FOR A 9IN (22.5CM) CAKE

5 oz (125g) plain chocolate

2 tbs water

5 oz (125g) unsalted butter

5 oz (125g) caster sugar

4 eggs and 1 egg white

2 oz (50g) self-raising flour

### filling

1½ lb (675g) canned morello cherries in syrup

1 tbs arrowroot

6 tbs kirsch

¾ pt (450ml) double cream

1 oz (25g) icing sugar

chocolate curls (p123)

Preheat the oven to 400°F/200°C/Gas 6. Butter a 9in (22.5cm) spring-form tin and sprinkle evenly with flour. Break the chocolate into small pieces and put into a bowl with the water. Melt over a pan of hot water and leave to cool.

Cream the butter and sugar until very pale and light. Separate the eggs and beat the yolks one at a time into the butter. Beat in the flour and then the melted chocolate. Whisk the egg whites to stiff peaks and fold into the cake mixture. Put into the prepared tin and bake for 40 minutes. Turn off the oven and leave the cake in for 5 minutes. Remove from the oven and cool in the tin for 15 minutes before turning on to a wire rack to finish cooling. When cold, cut the cake in half to make two layers and put the base on to a serving dish.

Drain the cherries and mix 2 tbs of the syrup with 2 tbs kirsch. Sprinkle over the cut sides of the cake layers. Mix the arrowroot with 3 tbs cherry syrup. Heat the remaining syrup just to boiling point. Mix with the arrowroot and then reheat gently until thick. Take off the heat.

Stone the cherries and reserve 12 for decoration. Stir the rest into the sauce with half the remaining kirsch. Leave until cold. Whip the cream and icing sugar to soft peaks and fold in the remaining kirsch. Spread the bottom cake layer with the cherry mixture and one-third of the cream. Add the top cake layer. Spread the remaining cream lightly all over the cake. Decorate with the reserved cherries and plenty of chocolate curls. Chill for 1 hour before serving.

# NÈGRE EN CHEMISE

☆☆

*A wonderfully rich steamed chocolate pudding, which gets its name from the dark centre in a 'shirt' of white cream.*

### INGREDIENTS

FOR 6

4 oz (100g) white bread without crusts
¼ pt (150ml) double cream
3 oz (75g) plain chocolate
4 oz (100g) unsalted butter
3 oz (75g) caster sugar
2 oz (50g) ground almonds
4 eggs
¼ pt (150ml) whipping cream
½ oz (15g) icing sugar

Grease a 2pt (1.2l) pudding basin. Break the bread into small pieces and put into a bowl with the cream. Leave to stand for 15 minutes and mash lightly with a fork. Break the chocolate into small pieces and put into a bowl over pan of hot water. Heat gently until melted.

Cream the butter and sugar until light and fluffy and beat in the almonds, eggs and melted chocolate. Gradually beat in the bread mixture until evenly coloured. Put into the prepared basin, cover with foil and steam for 2 hours.

Whip the whipping cream and icing sugar to soft peaks. Turn the pudding on to a serving dish. Spoon the cream over it and serve at once.

# CHOCOLATE ECLAIRS

☆☆

*This cunning combination of crisp light casing, sweetened cream and a dark chocolate glaze is perhaps the most indulgent of all chocolate based cakes.*

### INGREDIENTS

FOR 12 ECLAIRS

2½ oz (65g) plain flour

pinch of salt

2 oz (50g) butter

¼ pt (150ml) water

2 eggs and I egg yolk

filling and icing

½ pt (300ml) double cream

I egg white

½ oz (15g) icing sugar

6 oz (175g) plain chocolate

Preheat the oven to 400°F/200°C/Gas 6. Rinse two baking sheets in cold water. Sieve the flour and salt together. Put the butter and water into a pan and bring to the boil. Tip in the flour quickly and beat hard over low heat until the mixture is smooth; cook for I minute until it leaves the sides of the pan cleanly. Cool to lukewarm and then beat in the eggs a little at a time until the mixture is smooth and shiny. Make sure the baking sheets are still wet, and pipe the mixture into 3in (7.5cm) lengths on to them, leaving room for expansion. Bake for 25 minutes. Slit each éclair with a sharp knife and return to the oven for 5 minutes to dry out. Cool on a wire rack.

Whip the cream to stiff peaks. Whisk the egg white to stiff peaks and then whisk in the icing sugar. Fold into the cream. Slit right along the side of each éclair and fill with cream.

Break the chocolate into small pieces and put into a bowl over a pan of hot water. Heat until melted. Dip the top of each éclair into the chocolate and leave to set. Serve freshly baked.

❖

### Cook's tip for making éclairs

*It is important to follow the recipe very carefully to achieve perfect éclairs. Be sure not to open the oven door when baking. Don't fill and ice the éclairs until just before serving so that they retain their crispness.*

*Chocolate Eclairs*

## HOT CHOCOLATE SOUFFLÉ

☆

*An impressive but easy soufflé, which you can partly prepare up to 8 hours beforehand.*

### INGREDIENTS

FOR 4 6

4 oz (100g) plain chocolate

2 tbs water

½ pt (300ml) milk

1½ oz (40g) butter

1½ oz (40g) plain flour

¼ teasp vanilla essence

4 large eggs

2 oz (50g) caster sugar

icing sugar

Put the chocolate into a pan with the water and 2 tbs milk. Stir over low heat until the chocolate has melted and add the remaining milk. Bring to the boil and remove from the heat. Melt the butter over low heat and stir in the flour. Cook over low heat for 1 minute. Remove from the heat and add the hot milk. Return to the heat and bring to the boil, stirring well until thick. Add the vanilla essence and leave until cool. Separate the eggs, and beat the yolks and sugar into the chocolate sauce. (At this point, the mixture may be left for up to 8 hours.)

Preheat the oven to 375°F/190°C/Gas 5 with a baking sheet inside placed in the centre of the oven. Grease a 2pt (900ml) soufflé dish well with butter and sprinkle with a little caster sugar. Whisk the egg whites to stiff but not dry peaks and fold into the chocolate mixture. Pour into the prepared dish, and run a spoon round the edge of the mixture (this makes the soufflé rise with a 'cauliflower' top). Place on the hot baking sheet and bake for 40 minutes.

Sprinkle with icing sugar and serve immediately with cream.

## HELEN'S PANCAKE LAYER

☆☆

*Pears with chocolate form a classic combination, commemorated in the ice-cream confection* Poire Belle Hélène. *This is a hot blend of the same flavours.*

### INGREDIENTS

FOR 4–6

4 oz (100g) plain flour

pinch of salt

1 egg

½ pt (300ml) milk

filling

1½ lb (675g) ripe pears

¼ pt (150ml) water

1 oz (25g) caster sugar

4 oz (100g) plain chocolate

2 tbs lemon juice

2 oz (50g) hazelnuts

vanilla ice cream

whipped cream

Prepare the pancakes first by mixing together the flour, salt, egg and milk to make a creamy batter. Fry 8 thin pancakes in lard or oil, and keep hot. While the pancakes are cooking, prepare the filling. Peel the pears and cut into neat slices. Put into a pan with the water and sugar and simmer until tender. Drain and keep the pears warm. In another bowl, melt the chocolate with the lemon juice over hot water. Chop the hazelnuts finely and stir into the chocolate.

Place a pancake on a warm serving dish, cover with pears and pour over a little chocolate sauce. Continue in layers, finishing with a pancake.

Serve at once cut in wedges, accompanied by scoops of vanilla ice cream and spoonfuls of whipped cream.

# CHILLED CHOCOLATE SOUFFLÉ

☆☆

*A classic chocolate cream soufflé, standing high above the dish and decorated with cream and dark chocolate.*

### INGREDIENTS

FOR 4–6

¾ pt (450ml) milk

1½ oz (40g) cocoa powder

3 eggs

3 oz (75g) caster sugar

½ pt (300ml) double cream

½ oz (15g) gelatine

4 tbs water

2 oz (50g) plain chocolate

Take a 1pt (600ml) soufflé dish and tie round it a double band of greaseproof paper to stand at least 2in (5cm) above the rim. Grease the dish and paper lightly. Put the milk and cocoa into a pan and bring to the boil, stirring well. Separate the eggs. Beat the sugar and egg yolks together in a bowl and stir in the milk. Return to the pan and heat gently, stirring all the time until the custard thickens. Cool to lukewarm. Whip half the cream and stir into the custard. Put the gelatine and water into a cup and stand it in a pan of hot water. Stir the gelatine until syrupy. Cool to the same temperature as the custard and stir it into the chocolate mixture. When it is just beginning to set, whisk the egg whites to soft peaks and fold into the mixture. Pour into the prepared dish and leave until set.

Carefully peel off the paper band. Whip the remaining cream and spread half of it round the edge of the soufflé. Grate the chocolate coarsely and press round the cream-covered sides, covering the cream completely. Pipe the remaining cream in rosettes on top of the soufflé.

# CHOCOLATE ROULADE

☆☆

*A spectacular, delicious pudding which is easy to make. It must be made in advance, which is convenient for a dinner party.*

### INGREDIENTS

FOR 6

6 oz (175g) plain chocolate

5 eggs

6 oz (175g) caster sugar

2 tbs hot water

½ pt (300ml) double cream

icing sugar

Preheat the oven to 350°F/180°C/Gas 4. Oil a shallow 12x10in (30x25cm) tin and line with greaseproof paper.

Break the chocolate into small pieces and put into a bowl over a pan of hot water. Heat gently until melted. Separate the eggs and add the sugar to the yolks. Whisk until thick and pale. Cool the chocolate slightly and stir into the egg mixture. Stir in the hot water. Whisk the egg whites to stiff peaks and fold into the chocolate. Spread the mixture in the prepared tin and bake for 20 minutes. Cover with a piece of greaseproof paper and a cloth and leave overnight.

Put a piece of greaseproof paper on a flat surface and dust lightly with sieved icing sugar. Turn out the chocolate cake and remove paper. Whip the cream to soft peaks and spread lightly but evenly over the surface. Roll up like a Swiss roll (the surface may crack a little). Chill for 3 hours, and dust with sieved icing sugar.

*Chocolate Roulade*

about 25 minutes until firm. Turn on to a wire rack to cool.

Make the filling by melting half the chocolate in a bowl over hot water. Whisk in the cream to make a light cream. Grate the remaining chocolate. Remove the cream mixture from the heat and stir in the grated chocolate and liqueur.

Put one of the cakes on a serving dish and spoon on the cream filling. Chill for 1 hour.

Make the icing by mixing the sugar with hot coffee and then boiling until a little of the mixture dropped into a cup of cold water forms a soft ball. Remove from the heat. Melt the chocolate in a bowl over hot water, cool and then stir in the coffee syrup. Add the golden syrup, butter and Tia Maria. Mix very well and pour over the top of the second cake. Leave until completely cold and firm and then place this cake layer on top of the chocolate cream. Chill for 1 hour before serving.

## CHOCOLATE TRUFFLE

☆☆

*This blissful pudding, much loved by chocolate fans, needs a little care when preparing the chocolate cream mixture.*

### INGREDIENTS
FOR 8–10

4 oz (100g) soft margarine

4 oz (100g) caster sugar

4 oz (100g) self-raising flour

1 oz (25g) cocoa powder

2 eggs

1 tbs milk

syrup

2 oz (50g) caster sugar

4 tbs water

2 tbs rum or orange liqueur

chocolate cream

¾ pt (450ml) whipping cream

12 oz (350g) plain chocolate

cocoa powder

Preheat the oven to 350°F/180°C/Gas 4. Grease and base-line a 9in (22.5cm) round cake tin.

Put the margarine, sugar, flour, cocoa powder, eggs and milk into a bowl and beat hard until light and creamy. Put into the prepared tin and bake for 25–30 minutes until firm. Turn on to a wire rack to cool. Prepare the syrup by putting the sugar and water into a small, heavy-based pan and heating gently until melted. Boil for 2 minutes, take off heat and stir in the rum or orange liqueur.

Place the cake on a serving dish. Cool the syrup and sprinkle all over the cake.

Whip the cream to soft peaks. Melt the chocolate in a bowl over hot water. Cool until still running easily but not hot. Pour on to the cream, mixing well until evenly coloured. Spoon over the cake. Refrigerate for 2–3 hours and sprinkle well with cocoa powder.

❖

**Cook's tip for chocolate cream**

*Watch the temperature of the chocolate – if it is too hot it will cook and curdle the cream, but if it is too cool it will not blend easily into the cream. The texture should be like smooth whipped chocolate cream.*

# FUDGE POTS

☆

*Little pots of soft chocolate fudge are wonderful served with whipped cream.*

### INGREDIENTS

FOR 6

8 oz (225g) plain chocolate

4 eggs

4 oz (100g) unsalted butter

2 teasp caster sugar

Break the chocolate into small pieces and put into a bowl over hot water. Heat gently until melted. Separate the eggs and beat the yolks into the hot chocolate. Cut the butter into small pieces and add gradually to the chocolate, stirring well until evenly blended. Remove from the heat and cool for 6 minutes. Whisk the egg whites to stiff peaks and whisk in the sugar. Fold into the chocolate mixture until evenly coloured. Divide among 6 individual ramekins or glasses. Chill for 24 hours. Serve with whipped cream.

# CHOCOLATE CRACKLING FLAN

☆ ☆

*A crunchy flan case contrasts with a creamy chocolate filling and meringue topping.*

### INGREDIENTS

FOR 6

6 oz (175g) ground almonds

2 oz (50g) caster sugar

1 teasp rum

1 egg white

### filling and topping

8 oz (225g) plain chocolate

8 fl oz (225ml) double cream

1 egg yolk

1 tbs icing sugar

1 tbs rum

4 egg whites

4 oz (100g) caster sugar

1 oz (25g) flaked almonds

Butter an 8in (20cm) flan tin.

Stir together the almonds, sugar and rum until evenly coloured. Whisk the egg white to soft peaks and stir into the dry ingredients. Form into a ball, wrap in film and chill for 30 minutes. Preheat the oven to 350°F/180°C/Gas 4.

Roll out the dough on a lightly floured board and press into the prepared tin, patching the delicate dough if necessary. Cut a strip of foil to fit round the inside edge of the dough and press lightly to keep the dough firm. Bake for 25 minutes. Leave until cold and carefully remove the foil and the tin. Place the case on an ovenware serving plate.

To make the filling and topping, break the chocolate into small pieces and put into a bowl with the cream. Put over a pan of hot water and heat gently, stirring well until the mixture is smooth and thick. Take off the heat and leave to stand for 5 minutes. Stir in the egg yolk, icing sugar and rum and beat until light and fluffy. Pour into the flan case.

Whisk the egg whites to stiff peaks. Gradually beat in the sugar until firm and glossy. Spread over the chocolate filling to cover completely. Sprinkle with the flaked almonds. Bake at 450°F/230°C/Gas 8 for 5 minutes. Serve freshly baked.

# WHITE CHOCOLATE TERRINE

☆☆

*A moulded white chocolate mousse which is particularly delicious served with fresh summer fruit such as strawberries or raspberries.*

### INGREDIENTS

FOR 6

1 teasp gelatine

7 tbs water

2 tbs clear honey

10 oz (300g) white chocolate

pinch of salt

3 egg yolks

12 fl oz (350ml) whipping cream

Rinse a 1lb (450g) loaf tin in cold water and keep on one side. Put the gelatine and 2 tbs water into a cup and stand in a pan of hot water. Heat gently until the gelatine is syrupy. Put the honey into a heavy-based pan and add the remaining water. Bring to the boil and take off the heat. Break the chocolate into small pieces and stir into the honey. Add the gelatine and salt and stir until smooth. Stir in the egg yolks. Whip the cream to soft peaks and fold into the chocolate mixture. Spoon into the prepared tin and chill for 24 hours. Turn on to a serving dish and slice thickly to serve with fruit or with Chocolate Sauce (p111).

*White Chocolate Terrine*

# CHOCOLATE PAVLOVA

☆☆

*Pavlova is an Australian version of meringue cake, with a crisp surface and marshmallow-like centre. Filled with chocolate cream, it is delicious served with fresh strawberries or raspberries.*

### INGREDIENTS

FOR 6

3 egg whites

8 oz (225g) caster sugar

1 oz (25g) cocoa powder

1 oz (25g) cornflour

1 teasp white vinegar

½ pt (300ml) whipping cream

2 oz (50g) plain chocolate

few drops of vanilla essence

8 oz (225g) fresh strawberries or raspberries

icing sugar

Preheat the oven to 225°F/110°C/Gas ¼. Line a baking sheet with baking parchment and draw an 8In (20cm) circle in the centre.

Whisk the egg whites to stiff peaks and gradually whisk in half the sugar until stiff and glossy. Sieve the cocoa powder and cornflour together and fold into the meringue with the remaining sugar and the vinegar.

Spoon the meringue on to the circle and slightly scoop the centre of the meringue with the back of a spoon to form a slight well. Bake for 3 hours, turn off the oven and leave until cold. Carefully remove the meringue from baking parchment and place on a serving dish.

Just before serving, whip the cream to soft peaks. Grate the chocolate finely. Fold into the cream with the essence and spoon into the centre of the meringue. Top with a layer of fruit and sprinkle lightly with icing sugar.

## DARK CHOCOLATE ICE CREAM

☆

*A deeply flavoured ice which is delicious on its own, or used as a base for a sundae with sauce, nuts and whipped cream.*

### INGREDIENTS

FOR 6

1 pt (600ml) creamy milk

5 oz (125g) caster sugar

4 oz (100g) plain chocolate

3 oz (75g) cocoa powder

½ pt (300ml) double cream

Put the milk and sugar into a heavy-based pan and just bring to the boil. Take off the heat and add the chocolate broken into small pieces. Stir until well mixed. Whisk in the cocoa powder and return to heat for 2 minutes. Leave until cold, stirring occasionally. Whip the cream to soft peaks and fold in the chocolate mixture. Freeze for 1½ hours until half-frozen and beat well until smooth. Freeze again for 1 hour, beat again, and freeze until firm

## CHOCOLATE GRANITA

☆

*An ice which has the texture of frozen snow, and which looks exciting served in tall glasses topped with whipped cream.*

### INGREDIENTS

FOR 4

8 oz (225g) sugar

½ pt (300ml) water

4 oz (100g) plain chocolate

Put the sugar and half the water into a heavy-based pan and heat gently until the sugar has dissolved. Bring to the boil without stirring and simmer for about 5 minutes to make a syrup. Add the remaining water and the chocolate broken into small pieces and stir until the chocolate has melted. Leave for 1½ hours until cold and pour into a freezing tray. Freeze to a firm mush, stirring once or twice. To serve, spoon into tall glasses and top with whipped cream.

## WHITE CHOCOLATE ICE CREAM

☆

*For those who like a sweet chocolate flavour, this ice cream is good served with Dark Chocolate Rum Sauce (p113) or Raspberry Liqueur Sauce (p115).*

### INGREDIENTS

FOR 6

½ pt (300ml) single cream

4 oz (100g) white chocolate

2 oz (50g) caster sugar

6 egg yolks

Put the cream into a heavy-based pan with the chocolate and sugar. Heat gently until the chocolate has melted. Whisk the egg yolks in a bowl. Slowly pour on the chocolate and whisk until well blended. Return to the pan and heat gently until smooth and thick, but do not boil. Leave until cold and freeze for 3 hours, stirring twice during freezing.

# FROZEN CHOCOLATE SOUFFLÉ

☆☆

*A spectacular-looking and very light ice, which may be served with a sauce (pp111-15) and small sweet biscuits.*

## INGREDIENTS

FOR 6

3 eggs

2 oz (50g) caster sugar

4 oz (100g) plain chocolate

¾ pt (450ml) double cream

plain chocolate and icing sugar

Prepare a 1pt (600ml) soufflé dish by tying a double piece of greaseproof paper round the dish to stand 2in (5cm) above the rim.

Separate the eggs and put the yolks and sugar into a bowl over a pan of hot water. Whisk until the sugar has dissolved and the mixture forms thick ribbons. Melt the chocolate in a bowl over hot water and then whisk into the egg mixture until cool. Whip the cream to soft peaks and fold into the chocolate mixture. Whisk the egg whites to stiff peaks and fold into the mixture until evenly coloured. Spoon into the prepared dish and freeze for 4 hours.

To serve, remove the paper. Grate some plain chocolate coarsely and sprinkle over the top surface, then dust lightly with icing sugar.

# PEPPERMINT CREAM ICE

☆

*Chocolate and peppermint combine in an ice cream with a slightly crunchy texture. Serve each portion decorated with a thin peppermint cream.*

## INGREDIENTS

FOR 6

4 egg yolks

6 oz (175g) caster sugar

½ pt (300ml) milk

4 oz (100g) plain chocolate

2 tbs crème de menthe

3 oz (75g) chocolate mint crisps

½ pt (300ml) double cream

Whisk the egg yolks and sugar together until very pale and creamy. Heat the milk and chocolate in a heavy-based pan until just boiling. Gently pour on to the egg mixture, whisking all the time. Return to the pan and cook over gentle heat until thick and creamy. Remove from the heat and leave until cold. Stir in crème de menthe. Grate the chocolate mint crisps and fold into the chocolate mixture.

Whip the cream to soft peaks and fold into the chocolate custard. Freeze for 1½ hours until half-frozen. Beat well and return to the freezer for 1½ hours, beating once more during freezing.

## NUTTY CHOCOLATE TERRINE

☆

*A rich chocolate ice studded with three kinds
of nuts and made in a loaf shape for easy slicing.
Serve with Crème Anglaise (p115) or
Dark Chocolate Rum Sauce (p113).*

### INGREDIENTS

FOR 8

8 oz (225g) caster sugar

6 egg yolks

8 oz (225g) plain chocolate

1 pt (600ml) whipping cream

3 oz (75g) walnuts

3 oz (75g) hazelnuts

3 oz (75g) flaked almonds

Whisk the sugar and egg yolks together until very pale and creamy. Break the chocolate into small pieces and melt in a bowl over a pan of hot water. Cool slightly and fold into the whisked mixture. Whip the cream to soft peaks and fold into the chocolate. Chop the walnuts and hazelnuts and add all the nuts to the mixture. Line a 2lb (900g) loaf tin with foil and spoon in the mixture. Cover and freeze for 6 hours. To serve, leave to stand in the refrigerator for 30 minutes, turn out and peel off the foil. Cut into slices and place each serving on a pool of the chosen sauce.

## FROZEN MOCHA MOUSSE

☆

*A very light iced mousse which may be prepared
up to 10 days in advance.*

### INGREDIENTS

FOR 6

4 oz (100g) plain chocolate

1 tbs cocoa powder

1 teasp coffee powder

2 tbs boiling water

6 egg whites

3 oz (75g) caster sugar

grated plain chocolate

Break the chocolate into pieces and put into a bowl over a pan of hot water. Heat gently until melted. Mix the cocoa powder, coffee powder and water to a paste and stir into the chocolate, mixing well until thick and creamy.

Whisk the egg whites to stiff peaks. Gradually add the sugar, whisking all the time until the mixture is glossy. Fold in the chocolate mixture until thoroughly blended. Spoon into 6 ramekins. Place on a metal tray, and cover with freezer film. Freeze for 2 hours until firm. Store in the freezer for up to 10 days. Serve frozen with a sprinkling of grated chocolate.

*Overleaf: Coffee Truffle Bombe
with Mocha Cream Sauce*

# CHOCOLATE PARKIN

☆

*The rich gingerbread which is traditionally eaten on
Guy Fawkes' Day tastes very special when
combined with chocolate.*

### INGREDIENTS

FOR A 6IN (15CM) SQUARE CAKE

4 oz (100g) butter
4 oz (100g) black treacle
4 oz (100g) dark soft brown sugar
½ teasp bicarbonate of soda
6 tbs milk
4 oz (100g) plain flour
4 oz (100g) fine oatmeal
I teasp ground ginger
I teasp ground mixed spice
pinch of salt
I egg
4 oz (100g) plain chocolate

Preheat the oven to 325°F/160°C/Gas 3. Grease and base-line a 6in (15cm) square cake tin. Put the butter, treacle and sugar into a pan and heat gently until the fat has melted. Leave to cool. Stir the bicarbonate of soda into the milk. Stir the flour, oatmeal, ginger, spice and salt together. Beat in the butter mixture, milk and egg. Chop the chocolate finely and stir into the cake mixture. Put into the prepared tin and bake for I hour. Cool in the tin for 5 minutes and turn on to a wire rack to finish cooling. Store in a tin for 3 days before using.

# CHOCOLATE MARBLE CAKE

☆

*An old-fashioned nursery cake which is simple
to make but looks spectacular.*

### INGREDIENTS

FOR A 7IN (17.5CM) CAKE

8 oz (225g) soft margarine
8 oz (225g) caster sugar
few drops of vanilla essence
3 large eggs
10 oz (300g) self-raising flour
3 oz (75g) plain chocolate

Preheat the oven to 350°F/180°C/Gas 4. Grease and base-line a 7in (17.5cm) round cake tin. Cream the fat, sugar and essence until light and fluffy. Beat the eggs lightly together. Sieve the flour. Add the eggs and flour alternately to the creamed mixture.

Put half the mixture into another bowl. Melt the chocolate in a bowl over hot water and beat into half the mixture. Put alternate spoonfuls of plain and chocolate mixture into the prepared tin. Bake for 45 minutes. Cool in the tin for 2–3 minutes and turn on to a wire rack to cool.

*Chocolate Marble Cake*

## RICH DARK CHOCOLATE CAKE

☆

*The unusual addition of Guinness results in a chocolate cake which is very dark but light-textured.*

### INGREDIENTS

FOR AN 8IN (20CM) CAKE

4 oz (100g) soft margarine

6 oz (175g) dark soft brown sugar

2 eggs

6 oz (175g) plain flour

1 teasp baking powder

½ teasp bicarbonate of soda

¼ pt (150ml) Guinness

2 oz (50g) cocoa powder

filling and icing

4 oz (100g) plain chocolate

1 tbs milk

4 oz (100g) soft margarine

8 oz (225g) icing sugar

walnut halves

Preheat the oven to 350°F/180°C/Gas 4. Grease and base-line two 8in (20cm) sandwich tins.

Cream the fat and sugar until light and fluffy. Beat the eggs lightly. Sieve the flour, baking powder and soda. Add the eggs and flour alternately to the creamed mixture, beating well between each addition. Mix the Guinness and cocoa powder together to make a thick paste. Stir into the cake mixture and beat just enough to mix. Divide between the tins and bake for 30 minutes. Cool on a wire rack.

To make the icing, put the chocolate and milk into a bowl over a pan of hot water. When the chocolate has melted, remove from the heat and cool to lukewarm. Cream the fat and sugar together and beat in the chocolate until evenly coloured. Use one-third of the icing to put the two cake halves together. Swirl the remaining icing on top and decorate with walnut halves.

## BRAZILIAN CHOCOLATE CAKE

☆

*Nuts, dates and cherries combine with chocolate chips in a cut-and-come-again cake which needs no decoration.*

### INGREDIENTS

FOR A 2LB (900G) LOAF CAKE

4 oz (100g) dates

8 oz (225g) Brazil nuts

2 oz (50g) glacé cherries

4 oz (100g) chocolate chips

4 oz (100g) plain flour

½ teasp baking powder

pinch of salt

5½ oz (150g) sugar

3 eggs

Preheat the oven to 375°F/190°C/Gas 5. Grease and base-line a 2lb (900g) loaf tin.

Reserve 6 dates and 6 nuts and chop the rest roughly. Put into a bowl. Cut the cherries in half and add to the bowl with the chocolate chips. Sieve the flour, baking powder and salt and add to the bowl with the sugar. Stir well. Separate the eggs and whisk the whites until frothy. Stir in the yolks and add to the bowl. Mix well and put into the prepared tin. Arrange reserved dates and nuts on top. Bake for 1½ hours. Turn on to a wire rack to cool.

# CHOCOLATE FUDGE LAYER CAKE

☆☆

*A dark, dense chocolate cake with creamy fudge filling and topping – lovely for tea, or as a pudding.*

### INGREDIENTS

FOR AN 8IN (20CM) CAKE

4 oz (100g) plain chocolate

3 tbs boiling water

7 oz (200g) self-raising flour

1 oz (25g) cocoa powder

6 oz (175g) unsalted butter

6 oz (175g) caster sugar

1 teasp vanilla essence

4 eggs

2 tbs milk

### filling and topping

7 oz (200g) plain chocolate

6 fl oz (175ml) evaporated milk

8 oz (225g) icing sugar

Preheat the oven to 350°F/180°C/Gas 4. Grease and base-line two 8in (20cm) sandwich tins.

Break the chocolate into small pieces and put into a bowl with the water over hot water. Heat gently until melted. Sieve the flour and cocoa together. Cream the butter and sugar until soft and fluffy. Add the essence and chocolate. Separate the eggs and beat the yolks into the chocolate mixture. Fold in the flour mixture and milk. Whisk the egg whites to stiff peaks and fold into the mixture. Divide between the tins and bake for 30 minutes. Turn out on to a wire rack to cool.

To make the filling, melt the chocolate in a bowl over a pan of hot water. Add the evaporated milk and beat over the heat until light and creamy. Remove from the heat and leave to cool for 5 minutes, stirring often. Sieve the icing sugar and work into the chocolate mixture. When thick and smooth, sandwich the cakes together with one-third of the icing. Spread the rest over the surface of the cake.

# CHOCOLATE TEABREAD

☆

*This chocolate-flavoured fruit loaf may be eaten plain, or is even more delicious spread with unsalted butter.*

### INGREDIENTS

FOR A 2LB (900G) LOAF CAKE

9 oz (250g) self-raising flour

4 oz (100g) butter or hard margarine

4 oz (100g) caster sugar

2 oz (50g) seedless raisins

2 oz (50g) currants

1 oz (25g) chopped mixed peel

2 eggs

2 oz (50g) plain chocolate

3–4 tbs milk

Preheat the oven to 350°F/180°C/Gas 4. Grease and base-line a 2lb (900g) loaf tin. Sieve the flour into a bowl. Rub in the fat until the mixture is like fine breadcrumbs. Stir in the sugar, raisins, currants and peel. Beat the eggs lightly and stir into the mixture. Melt the chocolate in a pan over hot water and add to the mixture. Beat well, adding enough milk to make a soft dropping consistency. Put into the prepared tin and bake for 1 hour. Cool in the tin for 3 minutes and turn on to a wire rack to cool.

# CHOCOLATE BABA

☆☆

*A glorious confection for a special teatime, or for the end of a meal. This cake looks spectacular on a buffet table, but needs to be prepared the day before.*

## INGREDIENTS

FOR 8–10

4 oz (100g) seedless raisins

2 oz (50g) chopped mixed peel

2 oz (50g) glacé cherries

4 tbs rum

8 oz (225g) plain flour

1 oz (25g) cocoa powder

2 teasp baking powder

½ teasp salt

5 oz (125g) light soft brown sugar

2 eggs

6 tbs corn oil

6 tbs milk

½ teasp vanilla essence

### syrup and topping

4 oz (100g) sugar

¼ pt (150ml) water

4 tbs rum

½ pt (300ml) whipping cream

chocolate shapes

Put the raisins and peel into a bowl. Chop the cherries and mix with the other fruit. Stir in the rum and leave to soak. Preheat the oven to 350°F/180°C/Gas 4. Grease a 2½ pt (1.5l) ring tin. Sieve the flour, cocoa powder, baking powder and salt into a bowl and stir in the sugar until evenly coloured. Separate the eggs, and put the yolks into a bowl with the oil, milk and essence and mix well. Add to the dry ingredients and beat well to a creamy batter. Whisk the egg whites to stiff peaks and fold into the mixture. Lightly stir in the raisins, peel, cherries and rum. Put into the tin and bake for 55 minutes. Leave in the tin for 5 minutes and turn on to a wire rack to cool.

Put the sugar and water into a heavy-based pan and bring them slowly to the boil. Simmer for 5 minutes and then take off the heat and stir in the rum. When the cake is cold, return it to the tin and spoon over the hot syrup. Cover and leave overnight.

Just before serving, whip the cream to soft peaks. Turn out the cake on to a serving dish. Pipe the cream in lines and decorate with chocolate shapes. Serve at once.

*Chocolate Baba*

# CHOCOLATE WHISKY CAKE

☆☆

*A wonderful blending of flavours make this a very rich and completely irresistible cake, which may be eaten at the end of a meal.*

### INGREDIENTS

FOR AN 8IN (20CM) CAKE

2 oz (50g) seedless raisins

4 tbs whisky

7 oz (200g) plain chocolate

2 tbs water

4 oz (100g) unsalted butter

3 eggs

5 oz (125g) light soft brown sugar

2 oz (50g) plain flour

3 oz (75g) ground almonds

pinch of salt

### icing

6 oz (175g) plain chocolate

6 fl oz (175ml) double cream

Put the raisins into a bowl with the whisky and leave to soak overnight. Preheat the oven to 350°F/180°C/Gas 4. Grease and line a loose-bottomed 8in (20cm) round tin. Break the chocolate into small pieces and put into a bowl with the water. Heat gently until melted. Cut the butter into small pieces, and add gradually to the chocolate, stirring until smooth. Remove from the heat.

Separate the eggs and beat the yolks and sugar until pale and fluffy. Slowly pour in the chocolate mixture, stirring well until evenly coloured. Stir in the flour, almonds, raisins and whisky. Whisk the egg whites and salt to stiff peaks and fold into the chocolate mixture. Place in the tin and bake for 35 minutes. Leave in the tin for 5 minutes, and remove the sides of the tin. Gently slide the cake from its base on to a wire rack to cool. When cold, carefully peel off the lining paper and put the cake on to a serving plate.

To make the icing, break the chocolate into a bowl and add the cream. Heat gently over a pan of hot water until just melted. Stir until smooth, cool slightly and pour over the cake.

# CHOCOLATE HAZELNUT CAKE

☆☆

*This moist-textured, rich chocolate nut cake, topped by a chocolate cream icing, may be served as a cake or pudding with cream.*

### INGREDIENTS

FOR A 7IN (17.5CM) CAKE

4 oz (100g) unsalted butter

4 oz (100g) caster sugar

3 eggs

4 oz (100g) plain chocolate

5 oz (125g) ground hazelnuts

1 oz (25g) plain flour

### icing

¼ pt (150ml) double cream

5 oz (125g) plain chocolate

8 Liqueur Truffles (p99)

Preheat the oven to 350°F/180°C/Gas 4. Grease and base-line a 7in (17.5cm) spring-form tin. Butter the base paper and dust lightly with flour.

Cream the butter and sugar until very light and fluffy. Separate the eggs and beat in the yolks one at a time. Melt the chocolate in a bowl over hot water and stir into the creamed mixture. Mix the nuts and flour until evenly coloured and fold into the chocolate. Whisk the egg whites to stiff peaks and fold into the mixture. Place in the prepared tin and bake for 1 hour. Leave in the tin for 5 minutes and turn on to a wire rack to cool.

To make the icing, put the cream into a heavy-based pan and heat to just under boiling point. Add the chocolate and stir until thick and smooth. Take off the heat, and stir well until very creamy. Put the cake on to a serving plate and pour over the icing. When set (after about 1 hour), decorate with Liqueur Truffles.

# TRIPLE CAKE

☆☆

*Three ways of using plain chocolate in a rich cake, with a sponge layered with smooth chocolate buttercream and topped with mocha cream icing.*

## INGREDIENTS

FOR A 6IN (15CM) CAKE

**3 eggs**
**3 oz (75g) caster sugar**
**2 oz (50g) plain chocolate**
**3 oz (75g) plain flour**

### filling

**2 oz (50g) caster sugar**
**4 tbs water**
**2 egg yolks**
**5 oz (125g) unsalted butter**
**1½ oz (40g) plain chocolate**

### icing

**4 tbs double cream**
**1 tbs strong black coffee**
**2½ oz (65g) plain chocolate**

Preheat the oven to 350°F/180°C/Gas 4. Grease and line a 6in (15cm) round cake tin. Grease the lining paper and dust lightly with flour. Separate the eggs and whisk the yolks and sugar until very pale and thick. Melt the chocolate in a bowl over a pan of hot water. Fold into the egg mixture. Whisk the egg whites to stiff peaks and fold into the mixture alternately with the flour. Put into the prepared tin and bake for 35 minutes. Cool in the tin for 5 minutes and turn on to a wire rack to cool.

Prepare the buttercream by putting the sugar and water into a heavy-based pan. Dissolve the sugar over low heat and cook over medium heat to 215°F/102°C or until a little of the mixture forms a thin thread from the spoon (see Cook's Tip, p.19). Whisk the egg yolks until thick and creamy and gradually whisk in the hot syrup until the mixture is fluffy and cool. Beat the butter in another bowl until light and creamy and gradually beat in the egg mixture until thick and shiny. Melt the chocolate in a bowl over hot water, cool and stir into the buttercream.

Split the cake into three layers and reassemble with the buttercream between each layer. Put the cream and coffee into a heavy-based pan and bring just to the boil. Break the chocolate into small pieces and stir into the cream until melted. Remove from the heat and continue stirring until cool and smooth. Pour over the cake and leave to stand for 15 minutes.

# CHOCOLATE LEMON BOURBONS

☆

*The traditional Bourbon biscuit is given extra flavour with ground almonds and a hint of lemon rind.*

## INGREDIENTS

FOR 12 BISCUITS

3 oz (75g) butter
3 oz (75g) caster sugar
3 oz (75g) plain flour
3 oz (75g) ground almonds
grated rind of 1 lemon
2 oz (50g) plain chocolate

### filling
2 oz (50g) butter
4 oz (100g) icing sugar
½ oz (15g) cocoa powder

icing sugar

Preheat the oven to 375°F/190°C/Gas 5. Grease two baking sheets.

Cream the butter and sugar until light and fluffy. Work in the flour, ground almonds and lemon rind. Melt the chocolate in a bowl over hot water. Cool slightly and work into the mixture. Roll out and cut into rectangles. Place on the baking sheets and prick each biscuit three or four times with a fork. Bake for 20 minutes. Cool on a wire rack.

To make the filling, cream the butter, icing sugar and cocoa powder together until smooth and light. Sandwich the biscuits together in pairs and sprinkle the top surfaces with sieved icing sugar.

# FLORENTINES

☆☆

*Crisp fruit and nut biscuits contrast with smooth dark chocolate. They are perfect for a wedding reception or special party.*

## INGREDIENTS

FOR 20 BISCUITS

3 oz (75g) blanched almonds
1½ oz (40g) glacé cherries
2 oz (50g) unsalted butter
3 oz (75g) caster sugar
1 oz (25g) flaked almonds
2 oz (50g) chopped mixed peel
2 tbs double cream
4 oz (100g) plain chocolate

Preheat the oven to 350°F/180°C/Gas 4. Line two baking sheets with baking parchment. Chop the blanched almonds and quarter the cherries. Put the butter into a pan and stir in the sugar. Bring slowly to the boil. Remove the butter from the heat and stir in the chopped and flaked almonds, peel, cherries and cream.

Put teaspoonfuls far apart on the baking sheets. Bake for 8–10 minutes until golden-brown. Neaten the edges with a knife to form circles. Cool slightly and lift on to a wire rack to cool.

Melt the chocolate in a bowl over a pan of hot water. Spread on the smooth side of the biscuits and mark with a fork in wavy lines. Leave for 15 minutes to set.

# CHOCOLATE RINGS

☆

*Rich chocolate biscuits dipped in plain chocolate are the
perfect accompaniment to milk or coffee, or they may be
used as a base for serving ice creams or sorbets.*

## INGREDIENTS

### FOR 36 BISCUITS

4 oz (100g) unsalted butter

4 oz (100g) caster sugar

1 egg

few drops of vanilla essence

8 oz (225g) plain flour

1 oz (25g) cocoa powder

6 oz (175g) plain chocolate

Preheat the oven to 375°F/190°C/Gas 5. Grease two baking sheets.

Cream the butter and sugar until light and fluffy. Beat in the egg and essence. Work in the flour and cocoa. Chill for 30 minutes, and roll out. Cut into 2½in (6.25cm) rounds. Remove centres with a small round cutter and re-roll until all dough is used. Bake for 15 minutes, and cool on a wire rack.

Put the chocolate into a bowl over hot water, and heat gently until melted. Dip each biscuit into the chocolate until coated, and place on a sheet of baking parchment until cold and set.

# CHOCOLATE CHIP RAISIN COOKIES

☆

*Tempting cookies which are particularly good eaten
freshly baked and still slightly warm.*

## INGREDIENTS

### FOR 15 COOKIES

4 oz (100g) butter

4 oz (100g) light soft brown sugar

2 oz (50g) caster sugar

1 egg

few drops of vanilla essence

6 oz (175g) plain flour

½ teasp salt

½ teasp bicarbonate of soda

4 oz (100g) plain chocolate chips

4 oz (100g) seedless raisins

Preheat the oven to 325°F/160°C/Gas 3. Grease two baking sheets.

Cream together the butter, brown sugar and caster sugar until light and fluffy. Beat in the egg and vanilla essence. Sieve the flour with salt and soda and work into the creamed mixture. Fold in the chocolate chips and raisins. Form into 15 balls and place at intervals on the baking sheets, allowing room for spreading. Press down lightly with a fork dipped in cold water. Bake for 18 minutes. Cool for 2 minutes and lift on to a wire rack to finish cooling.

## CHOCOLATE CHIP SHORTBREAD

*Traditional shortbread with contrasting pieces of chocolate and flaked almonds.*

### INGREDIENTS

FOR A 6IN (15CM) SHORTBREAD ROUND

4 oz (100g) unsalted butter

2 oz (50g) caster sugar

6 oz (175g) plain flour

2 oz (50g) rice flour or cornflour

4 oz (100g) chocolate chips

1 oz (25g) flaked almonds

icing sugar

Preheat the oven to 300°F/150°C/Gas 2. Butter and flour a flan ring and place on a greased baking sheet.

Rub together the butter, sugar, flour and rice flour or cornflour to make a smooth, firm paste. Work in the chocolate chips. Press into the flan ring and press down lightly with a fork. Sprinkle with flaked almonds. Bake for 40 minutes until very pale gold in colour. Leave to stand until cold. Lift on to a serving plate and dust lightly with icing sugar. For convenience of serving, the shortbread may be marked lightly into triangles before it cools.

## CHOCOLATE COCONUT BARS

*Useful cookies to have in the tin for emergencies, with the slightly crunchy base contrasting with smooth chocolate.*

### INGREDIENTS

FOR 12–16 BARS

4 oz (100g) unsalted butter

6 oz (150g) caster sugar

2 eggs

4 oz (100g) ground rice

4 oz (100g) desiccated coconut

4 oz (100g) sultanas

4 oz (100g) glacé cherries

6 oz (175g) plain chocolate

Preheat the oven to 325°F/160°C/Gas 3. Grease and base-line an 11 x 7in (27.5 x 17.5cm) tin.

Cream the butter and sugar together until light and soft. Beat in the eggs and then stir in the ground rice, coconut, sultanas and chopped cherries. Put into the prepared tin and bake for 30 minutes. Leave to cool in the tin.

Break the chocolate into small pieces and put into a bowl over a pan of hot water. When the chocolate has melted, pour over the base. Leave until cold and firm before cutting into bars and removing from the tin.

# WHITE CHOCOLATE FRUIT BARS

☆

*An incredible confection of dried fruit and mixed nuts held together by white chocolate and honey, which is good with after-dinner coffee.*

### INGREDIENTS

FOR 24 SQUARES

4 oz (100g) flaked almonds

8 oz (225g) chopped walnuts

8 oz (225g) desiccated coconut

4 oz (100g) currants

4 oz (100g) chopped dried apricots

1 oz (25g) plain flour

8 oz (225g) white chocolate

6 oz (175g) clear honey

6 oz (175g) apricot jam

2 tbs icing sugar

Preheat the oven to 325°F/160°C/Gas 3. Grease and base-line an 8x12in (20x30cm) tin and grease the lining paper.

Put the almonds, walnuts, coconut, currants, apricots and flour into a large bowl and stir well together. Break the chocolate into small pieces and put into another bowl over hot water. Heat until melted, and then mix with the honey and jam. Stir into the dry ingredients and spread evenly in the prepared tin. Bake for 50 minutes. Cool in the tin and then sprinkle with icing sugar. Cut into small squares and remove from the tin. Store in the refrigerator.

# CHOCOLATE MAPLE BARS

☆☆

*A simple chocolate cake stuffed with raisins and topped with an unusual chocolate and maple syrup icing.*

### INGREDIENTS

FOR 16 BARS

5 oz (125g) unsalted butter

4½ oz (115g) light soft brown sugar

2 eggs

2 oz (50g) plain flour

1 oz (25g) self-raising flour

1 oz (25g) cocoa powder

¼ teasp bicarbonate of soda

4 oz (100g) seedless raisins

½ teasp vanilla essence

icing

4 oz (100g) plain or milk chocolate

3 tbs maple syrup

Preheat the oven to 350°F/180°C/Gas 4. Grease and base-line an 8x12in (20x30cm) tin and grease the lining paper.

Cream the butter and sugar until light and fluffy. Beat the eggs lightly. Sieve together the flours and cocoa. Add the eggs and flour mixture alternately to the creamed mixture, beating well. Beat in the soda and raisins with the vanilla essence. Spread in the prepared tin and bake for 25 minutes. Leave to stand for 5 minutes.

For the icing, break the chocolate into small pieces in a heavy-based pan with the maple syrup. Heat gently until the chocolate has melted. Stir well and pour over the warm cake. Leave until cold before cutting into bars.

## RUM RAISIN TOFFEE BARS

☆☆

*A chocolate shortbread base is topped with rum flavoured toffee spiked with raisins and coconut and finished with soft chocolate icing.*

### INGREDIENTS

FOR 16 BARS

5 oz (125g) unsalted butter

4 oz (100g) caster sugar

4 oz (100g) plain flour

1 oz (25g) cocoa powder

toffee layer

14 oz (400g) can sweetened condensed milk

1 oz (25g) unsalted butter

1 tbs rum

4 oz (100g) seedless raisins

3 oz (75g) desiccated coconut

topping

5 oz (125g) plain chocolate

1 oz (25g) unsalted butter

Preheat the oven to 350°F/180°C/Gas 4. Grease and baseline an 8x12in (20x30cm) tin and grease the lining paper.

Cream the butter and sugar until light and fluffy. Sieve the flour and cocoa powder together and fold into the mixture. Press evenly into the prepared tin and bake for 20 minutes. Cool in tin for 10 minutes.

To make the toffee layer, put the condensed milk and butter into a heavy-based pan and bring to the boil, stirring all the time and then continue cooking for 10 minutes until the mixture is golden brown. Take off the heat and stir in the rum, raisins and coconut. Cool to lukewarm and spread on the cooked base.

To make the icing, put the chocolate and butter into a bowl over a pan of hot water and heat gently until melted. Remove from the heat, stir well and spread on the cool filling. Leave until cold and set before cutting into bars.

## PEANUT BROWNIES

☆

*Children's favourites, which are nourishing (and non-sticky) for the lunchbox or a mid-morning snack.*

### INGREDIENTS

FOR 16 SQUARES

5 oz (125g) unsalted butter

4½ oz (115g) dark soft brown sugar

2 oz (50g) plain chocolate

2 tbs peanut butter

2 eggs

4 oz (100g) unsalted roasted peanuts

3 oz (75g) self-raising flour

1 tbs icing sugar

Preheat the oven to 350°F/180°C/Gas 4. Grease and baseline an 8in (20cm) square tin, and grease the lining paper.

Put the butter, sugar and chocolate into a heavy-based pan and heat gently until the chocolate has melted. Cool to lukewarm. Beat the peanut butter and eggs in a bowl and add the chopped peanuts. Stir in the chocolate mixture and the flour. Pour into the prepared tin and bake for 30 minutes.

Leave in the tin for 5 minutes and turn on to a wire rack to cool. When cold, sprinkle with icing sugar and cut into squares.

# CHOCOLATE CROISSANTS

☆☆

*A special treat for French children is equally appreciated by adults for a leisurely breakfast with a good cup of coffee.*

## INGREDIENTS

FOR 8–10 CROISSANTS

6 fl oz (175ml) milk
½ oz (15g) fresh yeast or ¼ oz (7g) dried yeast
1 teasp caster sugar
10 oz (300g) bread flour
5 oz (125g) butter
4 oz (100g) plain chocolate
beaten egg for glazing

Warm the milk to lukewarm and mix with the yeast and sugar. Leave to stand until bubbling strongly. Sieve the flour into a warm mixing bowl and add the milk and 1 oz (25g) melted butter. Mix to a soft dough and knead lightly until smooth. Place in a lightly oiled bowl, cover with a cloth and leave in a warm place for about 30 minutes until doubled in size. Knead again and roll lightly into a rectangle three times as long as wide.

Soften, but do not melt, the remaining butter, and divide into three portions. Dot one portion over the top two-thirds of the dough. Fold the bottom third up and the top third down over the butter. Seal the edges and turn so that the folded edges are at the sides. Roll into a rectangle again and repeat the process twice more. Cover the dough and leave in a cool place for 15 minutes. Roll out thinly and cut into triangles with 9in (22.5cm) long sides and 6in (15cm) base. Cut the chocolate into as many short thick bars as there are triangles.

Place a piece of chocolate at the base of each triangle and roll up loosely from the base. Curl the ends round to form a crescent. Place on baking trays and leave in a warm place for 20 minutes until well risen. Brush with beaten egg and bake at 450°F/230°C/Gas 8 for 10–15 minutes until golden brown. Eat freshly made.

# 9

# SWEETMEATS AND PETITS FOURS

*C*HOCOLATE IS BOOMING. *Everywhere there are chocolate shops together with grocers and gift shops with speciality chocolate departments. It is easy to buy luxury chocolates as presents or as self-indulgence, and after-dinner coffee is rarely served without some delectable sweetmeat. The traditional chocolate square allowed to children after a meal has been transformed into the adult truffle, liqueur cream or smooth fudge.*

*Sweet-making is a delicate art, but it is not difficult to acquire. For a few confections such as fudge, a sugar thermometer is useful, though not essential. Most sweetmeats rely on careful melting of the chocolate, a combination of the most delicious complementary flavours and long setting in a cool place. It is important not to over-handle chocolate sweetmeats as they quickly lose their shine and their charm, and they are best placed in paper or foil sweet cases as soon as they are prepared. Those who want to make very professional-looking sweets can now buy moulds and dipping tools in kitchen shops, so that little handling is required.*

*These sweetmeats are not designed to last a long time, and they are so good that they will get little chance to do so. Use the best possible chocolate, fresh cream, unsalted butter and good flavourings, and make only a small batch which will be eaten quickly.*

# FRESH CREAM TRUFFLES

☆☆

*A light hand and scrupulous attention to detail will produce delectable truffles which must be eaten quickly.*

### INGREDIENTS
FOR 1¼LB (550G) TRUFFLES (ABOUT 24)

¼ pt (150ml) double cream

1 vanilla pod

1 egg yolk

1 oz (25g) caster sugar

1 lb (450g) plain chocolate

1 oz (25g) unsalted butter

1 teasp oil

Put the cream and vanilla pod into a small, heavy-based pan and bring to the boil. Remove from the heat, cover and leave to stand for 20 minutes. Take out the vanilla pod (which may be washed, dried and used again). Put the egg yolk and caster sugar into a bowl and whisk until pale and thick. Whisk in the cream and return to the pan. Heat very gently for 3 minutes until the mixture begins to thicken, but do not boil. Break 5oz (125g) plain chocolate into small pieces. Take the cream off the heat and stir in the chocolate until melted. Chill in the refrigerator for 1 hour. Soften the butter and whisk into the mixture. Scoop out small spoonfuls of the mixture in rough truffle shapes and place on a piece of baking parchment. Freeze for 1 hour until very firm.

Break the remaining chocolate into a bowl over a pan of hot water and heat gently until melted. Stir in the oil. Remove from the heat and cool to lukewarm. Spoon a thin layer of chocolate over each truffle. When the chocolate has set firmly, turn the truffles over. Melt and cool any remaining chocolate and spoon over the base of each truffle to coat completely. Chill in the refrigerator and eat freshly made.

❖

#### Cook's tip
*For speed, or if a lighter Fresh Cream Truffle is preferred, only use 5oz (125g) chocolate from the ingredients. When the prepared mixture has been shaped and frozen, simply toss lightly in cocoa powder just before serving.*

❖

# LIQUEUR TRUFFLES

☆☆

*Rich cream truffles flavoured with any favourite liqueur should be served freshly made.*

### INGREDIENTS
FOR 24 TRUFFLES

8 tbs whipping cream

12 oz (350g) plain chocolate

1 oz (25g) unsalted butter

2 tbs liqueur

Put the cream into a heavy-based pan and heat gently to just below boiling point. Remove from the heat. Break half the chocolate into small pieces and stir into the cream with the butter. Beat well until smooth and thick. Cool to lukewarm and stir in the liqueur. Beat thoroughly and chill until firm. Shape the mixture into balls and chill again.

Break the remaining chocolate into small pieces and put into a bowl over hot water. Put a cocktail stick into each truffle. Remove the chocolate from heat and dip in each truffle, Drain well and fit sticks into a large potato or grapefruit. Leave until set and remove the cocktail sticks.

## DOUBLE TRUFFLES

☆☆

*These truffles are a little fiddly to make but the contrast between the dark coating and creamy white interior is worth the trouble taken.*

### INGREDIENTS

FOR 18 TRUFFLES

2 teasp liquid glucose

4 tbs double cream

5 oz (125g) white chocolate

coating

7 oz (200g) plain chocolate

2 oz (50g) unsalted butter

3 tbs double cream

2 tbs rum or Grand Marnier

cocoa powder

Put the glucose and cream into a small pan and bring to the boil. Take off the heat and stir in the white chocolate broken into small pieces. Stir until the chocolate has melted and then chill in the refrigerator until firm. Form into 18 small balls and chill until very firm.

To make the coating, put the chocolate and butter into a bowl over a pan of hot water and heat gently until the chocolate has melted. Take off the heat and stir well. Add the cream and rum or Grand Marnier. Chill until just firm. Form the mixture into 18 balls and flatten each ball into a round disc. Place a white chocolate ball in the centre of each one and wrap the dark coating round it. Roll lightly in cocoa powder, and chill for 3 hours until firm. Store in the refrigerator.

## WHITE CHOCOLATE TRUFFLES

☆☆

*The sweet blandness of white chocolate is contrasted with kirsch and a mixture of fruit and nuts.*

### INGREDIENTS

FOR 6OZ (175G) TRUFFLES (ABOUT 15)

4 oz (100g) white chocolate

3 tbs double cream

2 tbs chopped mixed glacé fruit

1 oz (25g) blanched split almonds

1 tbs kirsch

icing sugar

Chop the chocolate into small pieces. Put the cream and chocolate into a bowl over hot water and heat gently until the chocolate has melted. Meanwhile, chop the glacé fruit very finely. Spread the almonds on a baking sheet and toast under a medium grill until just golden. Chop the almonds finely and mix with the fruit. Stir into the chocolate and add the kirsch. Chill in the refrigerator for about 3 hours until firm. Roll into small balls with the hands, and roll lightly in icing sugar. Store in the refrigerator.

*Assorted truffles*

## PARISIAN TRUFFLES

☆

*Rich little truffles which are easily made
for a dinner party.*

### INGREDIENTS

FOR 8oz (225G) TRUFFLES (ABOUT 20)

4 oz (100g) plain chocolate

4 oz (100g) unsalted butter

2 oz (50g) icing sugar

2 egg yolks

cocoa powder

Break the chocolate into small pieces and put into a bowl over a pan of hot water. Add the butter and heat gently until melted. Beat in the sugar and egg yolks, and continue cooking until thick. Cool and leave in a cold place overnight. Roll into small balls with the hands and roll lightly in cocoa powder. Store in the refrigerator.

## WALNUT TRUFFLES

☆

*Slightly crunchy truffles which seem to melt in the
mouth. Follow the method carefully or the sweets
will be too sticky to roll successfully.*

### INGREDIENTS

FOR 12oz (350G) TRUFFLES (ABOUT 30)

8 oz (225g) plain chocolate

2 oz (50g) unsalted butter

4 tbs double cream

2 oz (50g) walnuts

2–3 tbs drinking chocolate powder

Break the chocolate into small pieces and put into a bowl over a pan of hot water. Heat gently until just melted. Remove from the heat and stir in the butter and cream. Grind the walnuts in a blender and stir into the mixture. Leave until completely cold.

Scoop out teaspoonfuls of the mixture and form into balls with the hands. Place in a single layer on a sheet of baking parchment. Chill in the refrigerator and then roll the truffles lightly in drinking chocolate powder. Store in the refrigerator.

## CHOCOLATE ORANGE TRUFFLES

☆☆

*Rich but delicate creamy truffles wrapped
in dark chocolate.*

### INGREDIENTS

FOR 12oz (350G) TRUFFLES (ABOUT 24)

4 oz (100g) ground almonds

4 oz (100g) icing sugar

1 tbs Cointreau or Grand Marnier

2 tbs double cream

6 oz (150g) plain chocolate

Put the almonds into a bowl. Sieve in the icing sugar, and stir well until evenly coloured. Add the liqueur and cream and mix to a firm paste. Chill in the refrigerator for 20 minutes. Form into small balls. Break the chocolate into small pieces and put into a bowl over a pan of hot water. Heat gently until just melted. Use a teaspoon to dip the little balls until they are coated. Drain well and place on a sheet of baking parchment until cold and set. Place in paper sweet cases.

# RUM AND ALMOND TRUFFLES

☆

*Quickly made truffles which are perfect*
*with coffee after dinner.*

## INGREDIENTS

FOR 18 TRUFFLES

4 oz (100g) plain chocolate

4 oz (100g) ground almonds

1 oz (25g) caster sugar

2 tbs rum

2 oz (50g) blanched almonds

Break the chocolate into small pieces and put into a bowl over a pan of hot water. Heat gently until the chocolate has melted. Stir in the almonds, sugar and rum. Remove from the heat and cool for 10 minutes. Roll into small balls. Chop the blanched almonds finely, and roll each truffle in the nuts. Chill for 30 minutes and put into sweet cases.

# RUM TRUFFLES

☆

*The flavouring may be varied by using brandy or an*
*orange- or cherry-flavoured liqueur instead of rum.*

## INGREDIENTS

FOR 12oz (350G) TRUFFLES (ABOUT 24)

8 oz (225g) plain chocolate

2 oz (50g) unsalted butter

1 tbs caster sugar

1 tbs rum

1 tbs double cream

1 egg yolk

cocoa or chocolate vermicelli

Break the chocolate into small pieces and put into a bowl over a pan of hot water. Heat gently until just melted. Take off the heat and stir in the butter, sugar, rum, cream and egg yolk. Beat until thick and cool. Put into the refrigerator for 20–30 minutes until firm but not hard. Shape into small balls and roll in cocoa or chocolate vermicelli. Place in paper sweet cases.

# RICH ORANGE TRUFFLES

☆

*Oranges and dark chocolate are natural companions,*
*and in this recipe the truffles are richly flavoured with*
*an orange liqueur, fresh orange rind and candied peel.*

## INGREDIENTS

FOR 12oz (350G) TRUFFLES (ABOUT 30)

2 oz (50g) unsalted butter

5 tbs double cream

7 oz (200g) plain chocolate

1 egg yolk

2 tbs chopped mixed candied peel

2 tbs Grand Marnier or Cointreau

1 teasp grated orange rind

cocoa powder

Cut the butter into small pieces and put into a small, heavy-based pan with the cream. Heat gently until the butter has melted and the cream is bubbling. Take off heat and add the chocolate broken into small pieces. Leave until the chocolate has melted and stir well. Mix in the egg yolk. Chop the peel very finely and stir into the mixture with the liqueur and orange rind. Chill in the refrigerator for about 3 hours until firm. Roll into small balls with the hands. Roll lightly in cocoa powder and chill before serving. Store in the refrigerator.

# CHOCOLATE FUDGE

☆☆

*Chocolate fudge is always delicious, but extra flavour may be added with nuts, dried fruit or a little rum.*

### INGREDIENTS

FOR 1½LB (675G) FUDGE

1 lb (450g) sugar

6 fl oz (175ml) milk

2 oz (50g) plain chocolate

2 oz (50g) unsalted butter

few drops of vanilla essence

Put the sugar and milk into a thick-based pan. Chop the chocolate finely and add to the milk. Stir over a low heat until the chocolate and sugar have melted. Boil gently to 237°F/114°C (or until a little of the mixture dropped into a cup of cold water forms a soft ball), stirring occasionally to prevent burning.

Take off the heat and add the butter. Cool for 5 minutes and beat hard with a wooden spoon until the mixture loses its gloss. Pour quickly into an oiled 11x7in (27.5x17.5cm) tin. Mark into squares while still slightly soft. Leave until cold before cutting and removing from the tin.

# CHOCOLATE CINNAMON FUDGE

☆☆

*A rich fudge in which the chocolate is spiked with cinnamon to make a very sophisticated sweetmeat.*

### INGREDIENTS

FOR 2LB (900G) FUDGE

1½ lb (675g) sugar

½ pt (300ml) milk

6 oz (175g) plain chocolate

4½ oz (115g) unsalted butter

1½ teasp ground cinnamon

Put the sugar and milk into a heavy-based pan. Break the chocolate into small pieces and add to the pan with the butter. Heat gently until the sugar has dissolved, stirring well. Boil gently to 237°F/114°C (or until a little of the mixture dropped into a cup of cold water forms a soft ball), stirring occasionally to prevent burning.

Take off the heat and cool for 5 minutes. Add the cinnamon and beat hard with a wooden spoon until the mixture loses its gloss. Pour quickly into an oiled 11x7in (27.5x17.5cm) tin. Mark into squares while still slightly soft. Leave until set before cutting and removing from the tin.

## UNCOOKED CHOCOLATE FUDGE

☆

*A fudge for fainthearts who are worried about boiling sugar. This fudge stores well in a freezer and is useful for holiday periods.*

### INGREDIENTS

FOR 2LB (900G) FUDGE

8 oz (225g) plain chocolate

4 oz (100g) unsalted butter

1 egg

1 lb (450g) icing sugar

4 tbs sweetened condensed milk or double cream

Break the chocolate into small pieces and put into a bowl with the butter over a pan of hot water. Heat gently until melted. Beat the egg lightly in a bowl. Sieve the icing sugar and add gradually to the egg with the milk or cream and the chocolate mixture. Beat well and put into a lightly buttered 11x7in (27.5x17.5cm) tin. Chill in the refrigerator for 3 hours until firm and cut into squares. Store in the refrigerator or freezer.

For ease of freezer storage, pour the mixture into rigid non-metal containers and do not mark into squares. Cover with foil or a freezer bag for storage up to 3 months.

If liked, chopped nuts, dried fruit or grated orange rind may be added to the fudge.

## CHOCOLATE ORANGE CREAMS

☆☆

*Squares of creamy orange chocolate are easily made and are very good with coffee after dinner.*

### INGREDIENTS

FOR 1¼LB (550G) SQUARES (ABOUT 40)

3 oz (75g) caster sugar

2 egg yolks

2 oz (50g) unsalted butter

4 tbs double cream

juice of ½ orange

1 teasp grated orange rind

1 lb (450g) plain chocolate

2 oz (50g) candied orange peel

Put the sugar and egg yolks into a bowl and whisk together until light and creamy. Put over a pan of hot water and stir in the butter, cream, orange juice and rind. Stir over heat until thick, but do not let the mixture boil. Break 8oz (225g) chocolate into small pieces and stir into the mixture. When the chocolate has melted, stir in the finely chopped candied peel. Line an 8x10in (20x25cm) tin with baking parchment. Pour the mixture into the tin and leave until cold and set. Turn out on to a clean sheet of baking parchment and peel off the lining paper.

Break the remaining chocolate into small pieces and put into a bowl over hot water. Heat until just melted. Leave to cool for 5 minutes and then spread over the chocolate cream. Leave until set and mark into small squares. When completely cold and firm, cut into squares and place in paper sweet cases.

## PRALINE LOG

☆☆

*A mocha truffle mixture is formed into a log and then rolled in crushed almond praline before being cut into tempting slices.*

### INGREDIENTS

FOR 1LB (450G) SWEETS

6 oz (175g) plain chocolate

3 oz (75g) unsalted butter

1 oz (25g) caster sugar

1 tbs strong black coffee

1 tbs brandy

1 egg and 1 egg yolk

praline

3 oz (75g) blanched almonds

4 oz (100g) sugar

4 tbs water

Break the chocolate into small pieces and put into a bowl with the butter, sugar, coffee and brandy. Put the bowl over a pan of hot water and heat gently until the chocolate has melted. Take off the heat and cool for 5 minutes. Separate the egg and beat the two yolks into the chocolate mixture. Beat the egg white to stiff peaks and fold in. Cool and then chill for 3 hours. Shape into a log 2in (5cm) in diameter and chill again.

While the mixture is chilling, prepare the praline. Put the nuts on to a baking sheet and bake at 350°F/180°C/Gas 4 for 5 minutes. Put the sugar and water into a heavy-based pan and heat gently until the sugar has dissolved. Bring to the boil and cool to a light caramel colour. Stir in the nuts. Butter a 10in (25cm) tin or a marble slab. Pour the mixture into the tin or on to the slab. Leave until cold and break into pieces. Crush in a food processor or with a rolling pin, but do not reduce to powder.

Roll the chilled log in the praline to make a thick coating, and chill again until needed. Slice into about 30 pieces.

## CHOCOLATE TORRONE

☆☆

*A fudge-like sweetmeat containing crisp little nuggets of biscuit.*

### INGREDIENTS

FOR 12oz (350G) TORRONE

4 oz (100g) plain chocolate

4 oz (100g) unsalted butter

2 tbs icing sugar

2 tbs rum

2 eggs

2 oz (50g) ground almonds

4 tbs broken Petit Beurre biscuits

Line a 1lb (450g) loaf tin with foil, and brush lightly with oil.

Break the chocolate into a bowl over a pan of hot water and heat gently until melted. Remove from the heat and leave until lukewarm. Cream the butter and sugar until light and fluffy and work in the rum. Separate the eggs and beat the yolks into the mixture. Stir in the ground almonds, and gradually beat in the chocolate.

Whisk the egg whites to stiff peaks and fold into the mixture. Break the biscuits into pieces about the size of a pea and stir into the mixture. Put into the prepared tin and smooth the surface. Cover and chill in the refrigerator for 6 hours. Turn out on to a flat surface and cut into slices, then cut each slice in half. Store in the refrigerator.

# CHOCOLATE SNAPS

☆☆

*Tiny chocolate biscuit cones filled with chocolate liqueur cream are an exciting addition to the* petits fours *selection. If cream horn moulds are not available, roll the mixture round oiled wooden spoon handles like brandy snaps.*

## INGREDIENTS

FOR 15 SNAPS

1 oz (25g) plain chocolate

1 oz (25g) unsalted butter

2 tbs light soft brown sugar

1½ tbs clear honey

1 oz (25g) plain flour

### filling

¼ pt (150ml) double cream

1 tbs orange liqueur

1 tbs icing sugar

2 oz (50g) plain chocolate

Preheat the oven to 350°F/180°C/Gas 4. Cover two baking sheets with baking parchment. Put the chocolate, butter, sugar and honey into a small, heavy-based pan and heat gently until melted. Take off the heat and work in the flour. Drop teaspoonfuls of mixture on to the baking parchment, leaving room for spreading (for ease of working, bake only 2–3 snaps on each sheet at a time). Bake for 5 minutes until just setting round edges. Leave on the tray for 30 seconds, lift off with a palette knife and wrap at once around base of cream horn tins, or oiled wooden spoon handles. When cold and crisp, slip off the moulds. If liked, the snaps may be stored in an airtight tin for 24 hours before filling.

To make the filling, whip the cream, liqueur and icing sugar to soft peaks. Melt the chocolate in a bowl over hot water, cool and stir into the cream. Just before serving, pipe the chocolate cream into the biscuit cases.

# COLETTES

☆☆

*Classic chocolate creams to serve with coffee. They will store in the refrigerator for up to 7 days.*

## INGREDIENTS

FOR 24 COLETTES

1 lb (450g) plain chocolate

¼ pt (150ml) double cream

2 tbs rum or brandy

2 oz (50g) unsalted butter

24 hazelnuts

Take 48 paper sweet cases and put them together in pairs to make 24 thicker containers. Take 6oz (175g) chocolate and

put into a bowl over a pan of hot water. When the chocolate has melted, stir well and remove from the heat. Spread chocolate on the base and sides of the paper cases to form an interior chocolate case. Place on a tray and chill in the refrigerator until set.

Put the cream into a bowl over a pan of hot water. When the cream is almost boiling, add the remaining chocolate broken into small pieces. Stir until the chocolate has melted. Add the rum or brandy and butter, and continue stirring over hot water until the mixture is thick and smooth. Take off heat and leave until cool. Put into a piping bag fitted with a large star nozzle and pipe a whorl of chocolate cream into each case. Place a hazelnut on each one. Store in the refrigerator.

## CHOCOLATE ALMOND CRUNCH

☆☆

*Rich coffee-flavoured toffee packed with toasted almonds is covered with chocolate and more nuts.*

### INGREDIENTS
FOR 1½LB (675G) TOFFEE

6 oz (175g) blanched split almonds

8 oz (225g) caster sugar

6 oz (175g) unsalted butter

1 tbs coffee powder

1 tbs boiling water

4 oz (100g) plain chocolate

Place the almonds in a thin layer on a baking sheet and toast under a medium grill until just tinged with gold. Chop 2oz (50g) almonds and keep on one side. Put the sugar and butter into a thick-based pan. Dissolve the coffee in the water and add to the pan. Heat gently, stirring all the time until the sugar has dissolved. Boil gently to 280°F/138°C (or until a little of the mixture dropped into a cup of cold water separates into threads which are hard but not brittle).

Take off the heat and stir in the split almonds. Pour into an oiled baking tin and leave until cold. Put the chocolate into a bowl over a pan of hot water and heat until melted. Spread the chocolate over the toffee and sprinkle with chopped almonds. Leave until set and break the toffee into pieces.

## CHOCOLATE CHERRY CREAMS

☆☆

*These petits fours take a little care and time to make, but the results are delicious.*

### INGREDIENTS
FOR 24 CHOCOLATES

24 maraschino cherries

4 tbs brandy

8 oz (225g) plain chocolate

2 oz (50g) sugar

2 tbs water

2 oz (50g) unsalted butter

2 oz (50g) icing sugar

Put the cherries into a bowl and cover with the brandy. Leave to stand for 8 hours. Take 48 paper sweet cases and put them together in pairs to make 24 firmer cases. Break the chocolate into small pieces and put half of it into a bowl over a pan of hot water. Heat gently until just melted. Brush the chocolate fairly thickly inside the sweet cases to cover the sides and bases completely. Leave until cold and set.

Drain the cherries and place one in each chocolate case. Put the sugar and water into a thick-based pan and boil to a thick syrup. Add half the drained brandy, stir well and cool. Cover the cherries with this syrup. Cream the butter and icing sugar and remaining brandy, and pipe this mixture over the cherries. Chill in the refrigerator until cold and firm.

Grate 1oz (25g) chocolate and keep on one side. Melt the remaining chocolate over hot water, leave until almost cold, and pour over the sweets. Sprinkle with grated chocolate. Leave until cold and set before removing from the paper cases.

## CRAZY PAVEMENT

☆

*Quickly made and delicious, this sweetmeat provides a
contrast of flavours and textures as well as colours.*

### INGREDIENTS

FOR 1¼LB (550G) SWEETS

1 lb (450g) plain chocolate

12 pink and white marshmallows

3 oz (75g) walnuts

3 oz (75g) seedless raisins

Break the chocolate into small pieces and put into a bowl over
a pan of hot water. Heat gently until just melted. Chop the
marshmallows with kitchen scissors. Chop the walnuts roughly.

Line a baking tray with baking parchment. Remove the
chocolate from the heat and stir in the marshmallows, raisins
and walnuts until well coated. Pour into the tin and smooth
evenly. Leave until cold and hard, and break into pieces.

## CHOCOLATE PRALINES

☆

*Creamy nutty little chocolates which are an attractive
addition to a dish of petits fours.*

### INGREDIENTS

FOR 18 PRALINES

4 oz (100g) plain chocolate

2 oz (50g) unsalted butter

3 oz (75g) icing sugar

1 oz (25g) ground hazelnuts

1 teasp rum or coffee liqueur

18 crystallised violets

Break the chocolate into small pieces and put into a bowl
with the butter. Place over a pan of hot water and heat
gently until just melted. Remove from the heat and stir in the
sugar, nuts and liqueur. Beat well and then put the mixture
into a piping bag fitted with a star nozzle. Place 18 paper
sweet cases on a plate and pipe the mixture in a whorl into
each case. Top with a crystallised violet. Chill in the refrigerator for 30 minutes and serve freshly made.

## CHOCOLATE STRAWBERRIES

☆

*A colourful way of combining the sharpness of fruit
with the smooth richness of chocolate makes* petits fours
*for the end of a summer meal or a wedding reception.*

### INGREDIENTS

FOR 1LB (450G) *PETITS FOURS*

6 oz (175g) plain chocolate

1½ oz (40g) unsalted butter

6 tbs double cream

1 lb (450g) strawberries

Use fresh, ripe, firm strawberries and make sure that they are
very clean and dry; leave the green tops in place. Put the
chocolate into a bowl with the butter over a pan of hot
water. Heat gently until the chocolate has melted. Take off
the heat and stir in the cream. Leave until cool and just beginning to thicken.

Place a piece of baking parchment on a flat surface.
Hold each strawberry by its stalk and dip into the chocolate
until two-thirds covered. Place on the baking parchment.
Leave until completely cold and firm. Lift off the paper and
arrange on a serving dish.

## CHOCOLATE CRUNCHIES

☆

*Quickly-made little sweets which store well in a tin.*

### INGREDIENTS

FOR 1LB (450G) SWEETS (ABOUT 20)

8 oz (225g) plain chocolate

2 oz (50g) glacé cherries

2 oz (50g) angelica

2 oz (50g) sultanas

2 oz (50g) seedless raisins

2 oz (50g) walnuts

Break the chocolate into small pieces and put into a bowl over a pan of hot water. Heat gently until just melted. Chop all the other ingredients roughly. Remove the chocolate from the heat and stir in the fruit and nuts. Drop spoonfuls into paper sweet cases and leave until set.

## CHOCOLATE COCONUT ICE

☆

*Coconut ice is a very old-fashioned sweetmeat but is rather unusual when flavoured with chocolate.*

### INGREDIENTS

MAKES 1¼LB (550G) COCONUT ICE

1 lb (450g) granulated sugar

¼ pt (150ml) milk

2 tbs cocoa powder

4 oz (100g) desiccated coconut

Put the sugar, milk and cocoa powder into a heavy saucepan. Stir well and boil for 5 minutes. Take off the heat and stir in the coconut. Beat hard for 1 minute and pour into a tin rinsed in cold water. Leave until cold before cutting into squares or bars.

## ORANGE THINS

☆

*Flavoured chocolate morsels to serve with after-dinner coffee.*

### INGREDIENTS

FOR 10OZ (300G) SWEETS

8 oz (225g) plain chocolate

2 oz (50g) unsalted butter

1 teasp grated orange rind

2 tbs orange liqueur

Line an 8in (20cm) square cake tin with foil and brush the foil lightly with flavourless oil. Put the chocolate and butter into a bowl over a pan of hot water and heat gently until just melted. Remove from the heat and stir in the orange rind and liqueur. Pour into the lined tin. Cover and chill until set. Turn out of the pan and cut into squares or triangles. Keep in the refrigerator before serving.

*Coffee Thins* Substitute 1 teasp instant coffee powder and 2 tbs coffee liqueur for the orange rind and liqueur.

# 10

# SAUCES

*A SMOOTH SAUCE provides a professional finish to a dish, producing a flavour which intensifies or enhances a pudding, a texture which adds richness and a colour which improves appearances. Even simple custard or flavoured cream can provide the perfect partner for a chocolate pudding. On the other hand a very dark and syrupy chocolate sauce, coffee sauce or a contrasting fruit sauce will provide a most sophisticated blending of flavours, colours and textures. Try a sauce with almost any hot or cold pudding or ice – even mousses and soufflés benefit from the contrast. Chocolate addicts may care to make up a large quantity of chocolate sauce and store it in the refrigerator or freezer to use with everything.*

## CHOCOLATE SAUCE

☆

*A quickly made sauce which is richly flavoured and glossy. It will thicken as it cools, and should be stirred occasionally. Serve it hot or cold, or store in the freezer for emergencies.*

### INGREDIENTS
FOR 4–6
¼ pt (150ml) water
4 oz (100g) caster sugar
2 oz (50g) cocoa powder

Put the water and sugar into a pan and heat gently until the sugar has dissolved. Bring to the boil and simmer for 1 minute. Whisk in the cocoa and bring back to the boil, whisking hard until the sauce is smooth.

## MOCHA CREAM SAUCE

☆

*This rich, creamy chocolate sauce spiked with coffee and brandy may be served hot or cold.*

### INGREDIENTS
FOR ¾ PT (450ML) SAUCE
½ pt (300ml) double cream
1 tbs strong black coffee
8 oz (225g) plain chocolate
1 tbs brandy

Put the cream and coffee into a heavy-based pan and bring just to the boil. Break the chocolate into small pieces and add to the pan. Heat gently until the chocolate has melted. Take off the heat and add the brandy, stirring until smooth.

## CHOCOLATE WHIPPED CUSTARD

☆

*A light chocolate custard, which is very good with steamed puddings.*

### INGREDIENTS

FOR 4

½ pt (300ml) milk

1 tbs caster sugar

1 egg

1 oz (25g) plain chocolate

Put the milk and sugar into a small pan and bring to boiling point. Separate the egg and put the yolk into a bowl. Pour on a little of the hot milk and beat well. Strain back into the pan with the remaining milk and stir gently over low heat until thickened. Chop the chocolate finely and stir into the custard. Remove from the heat and cool slightly. Whisk the egg white to soft peaks and fold into the custard. Serve at once.

## CHOCOLATE MOUSSELINE SAUCE

☆

*Rich creamy sauce to serve with pancakes or light sponge puddings.*

### INGREDIENTS

FOR 4

2 eggs and 1 egg yolk

2½ fl oz (65ml) double cream

1½ oz (40g) caster sugar

2 tbs sweet sherry

2 oz (50g) grated plain chocolate

Put the eggs and egg yolk into a bowl with the cream, and place over a pan of hot water. Heat gently, beating until smooth and thick. Add the sugar and sherry and beat until the sugar has melted. Stir in the chocolate and remove from the heat.

## MOCHA SAUCE

☆

*Coffee-spiked chocolate sauce which will pair with mocha puddings or with chocolate ones.*

### INGREDIENTS

FOR 4

1 oz (25g) butter

1 oz (25g) plain flour

¾ pt (450ml) milk

1 tbs coffee essence

2 oz (50g) plain chocolate

1 tbs caster sugar

Put the butter into a pan and heat gently until melted. Stir in the flour and cook for 1 minute over low heat. Work in the milk and stir over low heat until smooth and creamy. Stir in the coffee essence and cook for 1 minute. Chop the chocolate finely and add to the sauce with the sugar. Stir until melted and serve at once. For added richness, stir 2–3 tbs cream into the sauce just before serving.

## DARK CHOCOLATE RUM SAUCE

*Luscious chocolate sauce to serve with hot puddings or with ice cream. If preferred, strong coffee may be used instead of water and the rum omitted.*

### INGREDIENTS
FOR 4–6
2 oz (50g) caster sugar
4 tbs water
4 oz (100g) plain chocolate
2 tbs rum
½ oz (15g) unsalted butter

Put the sugar and water into a small, heavy-based pan over low heat and stir until the sugar has dissolved. Bring to the boil. Take off the heat and add small pieces of chocolate, stirring well. Stir in the rum and butter and serve at once.

## CHOCOLATE BUTTERSCOTCH SAUCE

*A lightly flavoured chocolate sauce which is good with steamed or baked puddings or vanilla ice cream.*

### INGREDIENTS
FOR ½PT (300ML) SAUCE
2 oz (50g) unsalted butter
2 oz (50g) demerara sugar
1 oz (25g) drinking chocolate powder
6 fl oz (175ml) creamy milk

Mix the butter, sugar and drinking chocolate powder in a heavy-based pan, and stir over low heat until the butter has melted and the sugar has dissolved. Raise the heat and cook for 2 minutes. Take off the heat and stir in the milk until evenly blended. Bring to the boil and cook for 2 minutes. Serve warm or cold.

## CHOCOLATE MOUSSE SAUCE

*A rich, foaming sauce for ices, mousses and puddings.*

### INGREDIENTS
FOR 4
4 oz (100g) plain chocolate
1 oz (25g) butter
6 tbs water
2 eggs

Put the chocolate into a bowl with the butter and water and heat over a pan of hot water until just melted. Separate the eggs. Remove chocolate from heat and beat in the egg yolks. Whisk the egg whites to soft peaks and fold into the mixture. Serve at once.

## CHOCOLATE FUDGE SAUCE

☆

*A good sauce to serve hot or warm over puddings, mousses or ices.*

### INGREDIENTS

½ PT (300ML) SAUCE

6 oz (175g) can evaporated milk

3 oz (75g) plain chocolate

2 oz (50g) light soft brown sugar

1 oz (25g) butter

¼ teasp vanilla essence

Put the evaporated milk into a heavy-based pan. Break the chocolate into small pieces and add to the pan with the sugar and butter. Heat gently and stir continuously over low heat until the chocolate has melted and the sugar has dissolved, but do not boil. Remove from the heat and stir in the vanilla essence.

## COFFEE CUSTARD SAUCE

☆☆

*Coffee is the perfect complement to chocolate, and this rich custard is good with any dark chocolate pudding, whether hot or cold.*

### INGREDIENTS

FOR 1 PT (600ML) SAUCE

½ pt (300ml) milk

½ pt (300ml) single cream

1 oz (25g) coffee powder

4 egg yolks

3 oz (75g) caster sugar

Put the milk, cream and coffee powder into a heavy-based pan and bring to the boil. Whisk the egg yolks and sugar in a bowl until thick and creamy. Slowly pour the milk on to the eggs, whisking all the time. Return to the pan and stir gently over low heat until the mixture thickens and coats the back of a spoon. Strain and serve hot or cold.

## MINT CREAM

☆

*A perfect filling for chocolate pancakes or topping for a rich chocolate mousse or gâteau.*

### INGREDIENTS

FOR ½ PT (300ML) CREAM

½ pt (300ml) double cream

1 tbs caster sugar

3 tbs crème de menthe

Whip the cream to soft peaks. Add the sugar and continue whipping until the cream stands in stiff peaks. Stir in the crème de menthe until evenly coloured.

## MARS BAR SAUCE

☆

*The secret treat of generations of bed-sitter dwellers, this instant chocolate sauce tastes wonderful over ice creams and puddings. Simply chop two large Mars Bars and heat very gently in a small, heavy-based saucepan. When melted, stir well and use at once. For incredible richness, stir in a spoonful or two of thick cream just before serving.*

## RASPBERRY LIQUEUR SAUCE

☆

*Clear red fruit sauce is quickly made and provides a wonderful foil to chocolate dishes. Framboise, kirsch, cassis, rum or brandy may be used for the alcoholic content.*

### INGREDIENTS

FOR ½ PT (300ML) SAUCE

1 lb (450g) fresh or frozen raspberries

8 oz (225g) icing sugar

juice of ½ lemon

2 tbs liqueur

Sieve the fruit to make a purée. Stir in the sugar and lemon juice until the sugar has dissolved. Chill and stir in the liqueur just before serving.

## ORANGE SAUCE

☆

*Oranges go beautifully with chocolate, and this sauce helps to offset the richness of hot chocolate puddings.*

### INGREDIENTS

FOR ½ PT (300ML) SAUCE

2 oranges

½ pt (300ml) water

1 tbs unsalted butter

1 tbs plain flour

½ oz (15g) caster sugar

2 tbs orange liqueur

Grate the rind of the oranges and put into a heavy-based pan with the water. Bring to the boil and simmer for 10 minutes.

In another pan, melt the butter and work in the flour. Add the orange liqueur and simmer for 5 minutes, stirring well. Squeeze the juice from the oranges and strain into the pan. Add the sugar, stir well and simmer over low heat for 5 minutes. Remove from the heat and stir in the liqueur. Serve at once.

## CRÈME ANGLAISE

☆ ☆

*The French version of custard is thin, sweet and creamy, and is delicious cold with chocolate dishes.*

### INGREDIENTS

FOR 1 PT (600ML) SAUCE

½ pt (300ml) milk

vanilla pod

6 egg yolks

4 oz (100g) caster sugar

½ pt (300ml) single cream

2 teasp orange flower water

Put the milk into a heavy-based pan with the split vanilla pod. Bring to the boil. Take off the heat, cover and leave to stand for 10 minutes. Whisk the yolks and sugar together in a bowl until pale and creamy. Strain in the milk, whisking well. Put into a heavy-based pan and stir over low heat until the sauce coats the spoon. Remove from the heat and leave to cool, stirring frequently. When nearly cold, stir in the cream and orange flower water.

# DRINKS

*C*HOCOLATE IS AN ALMOST *universal comforter. There is nothing quite like a hot or cold chocolate drink to comfort, feed and yet stimulate. In warmer countries such as Mexico, they like their chocolate spiked with spices or contrasting coffee; in colder climates, the chocolate has to be lighter, sweeter and frothier, often served with cream or laced with spirits.*

*A smooth chocolate syrup is a good basis for cold chocolate drinks, quickly prepared with chilled milk or ice cream. For hot drinks, cocoa powder or drinking chocolate powder is now most easily used, although they were once prepared with melted, unsweetened chocolate in a long and laborious business.*

## CHOCOLATE NOG

☆

*An old-fashioned way of making a nourishing milk drink for a cold morning.*

### INGREDIENTS

FOR 2

¾ pt (450ml) milk

1 tbs caster sugar

1 vanilla pod

1 egg

3 oz (75g) plain chocolate

Put the milk, caster sugar and vanilla pod into a heavy-based pan and heat gently. When the milk is just at boiling point, remove from heat and take out the vanilla pod (this can be washed, dried and used again). Separate the egg, and whisk the egg yolk and milk together. Break the chocolate into small pieces and add to the mixture, stirring until creamy. Whisk the egg white to stiff peaks. Pour in the hot milk, whisking all the time. Pour into two warm mugs and serve at once. If liked, a blob of whipped cream may be placed on top of each serving.

# BASIC CHOCOLATE SYRUP

☆

*This syrup may be used as a sauce for puddings and ice creams, but it is useful to store in the refrigerator as the base for chocolate drinks.*

## INGREDIENTS

FOR ½PT (300ML) SYRUP

½pt (300ml) water

10 oz (300g) light soft brown sugar

4 oz (100g) cocoa powder

pinch of salt

2 teasp vanilla essence

Put the water into a heavy-based pan and stir in the sugar, cocoa powder and salt. Bring to the boil and then simmer for 5 minutes, stirring often. Remove from the heat and leave to cool, stirring occasionally. Stir in the vanilla essence. When cold, cover and store in the refrigerator.

# REAL COCOA

☆

*Real men like real cocoa, made in the traditional way, preferably with Dutch cocoa powder, which has the finest flavour.*

## INGREDIENTS

FOR 4

4 tbs cocoa powder

3 tbs sugar

pinch of salt

¼pt (150ml) boiling water

1½pt (900ml) milk

Mix the cocoa powder, sugar and salt in a heavy-based pan. Add the water and mix to a paste. Simmer for 3 minutes. Add the milk and heat slowly to just below boiling point. Whisk well and pour into hot mugs. If you are a sailor or wildfowler, add some rum.

# CHOCOLATE TODDY

☆

*A soothing bedtime drink with a very special flavour.*

## INGREDIENTS

FOR 2

1 pt (600ml) milk

2 oz (50g) plain chocolate

2–3 tbs rum

1 tbs double cream

pinch of ground nutmeg

Put the milk into a heavy-based pan. Break the chocolate into small pieces and add to the pan. Bring to the boil, stirring occasionally. Take off the heat and stir in the rum. Divide between two warm mugs. Pour the cream over the back of a teaspoon on to the hot chocolate, so that the cream floats on the surface. Sprinkle lightly with nutmeg and serve at once.

# SWISS CHOCOLATE

☆

*Richly warming and comforting, this is the drink for
a cold winter's night, or even for mid-morning
after a brisk walk.*

### INGREDIENTS

FOR 4

2 pt (1.2l) milk

4 heaped tbs drinking chocolate powder

¼ pt (150ml) double cream

pinch of ground cinnamon or cocoa powder

Heat the milk to boiling point. Take off heat and whisk in the drinking chocolate powder. Whip the cream to soft peaks. Pour the hot chocolate into mugs. Spoon cream on top of each mug and sprinkle lightly with cinnamon or cocoa powder.

# BREAKFAST CHOCOLATE

☆

*Thick hot chocolate makes a marvellous drink for a
winter breakfast, to accompany croissants, brioches
or a lightly fruited bun.*

### INGREDIENTS

FOR 2

3 oz (75g) plain chocolate

5 tbs boiling water

½ pt (300ml) creamy milk

Break the chocolate into small pieces and put into a heavy-based pan with the water. Heat gently, stirring well, until the chocolate has melted and the mixture is thick. Heat the milk in another saucepan. Divide the hot chocolate between two mugs and pour in the hot milk. Serve at once.

# MEXICAN CHOCOLATE

☆

*Almost a complete meal, this spiced chocolate drink
is very reviving in cold weather.*

### INGREDIENTS

FOR 4

1 pt (600ml) milk

½ pt (300ml) double cream

½ teasp ground cinnamon

½ teasp ground nutmeg

pinch of ground allspice

pinch of salt

2 oz (50g) plain chocolate

5 tbs water

2 egg yolks

Put the milk and cream into a bowl over a pan of hot water and bring just to the boil. Add the spices and salt, and simmer for 1 hour.

Just before serving, heat the chocolate and water in a small pan over low heat until the chocolate has melted. Take off the heat and beat in the egg yolks. Whisk in the spiced milk until the mixture thickens. Serve at once.

# CHOCOLATE MILK SHAKE

☆

*Refreshing milk shakes are best made with milk which has been chilled in the refrigerator and whirled up in a blender with flavouring.*

### INGREDIENTS

FOR 1

½ pt (300ml) milk

3 tbs Chocolate Syrup (p117)

2 tbs finely crushed ice

pinch of ground cinnamon or nutmeg

Put the milk, Chocolate Syrup and ice into a blender and whirl until well mixed. Pour into a chilled glass and sprinkle with cinnamon or nutmeg.

# CHOCOLATE ICE CREAM SODA

☆

*A quickly assembled summer drink, which is easily made if all the ingredients have been well chilled in the refrigerator. The ice cream may be chocolate, vanilla or mint-flavoured.*

### INGREDIENTS

FOR 1

3 tbs Chocolate Syrup (p117)

1 tbs double cream

1 scoop ice cream

soda water

Put the Chocolate Syrup and cream into a tall glass and stir until well mixed. Add the ice cream and top up with soda water. Stir thoroughly and serve at once with a straw and long spoon.

# MOCHA COOLER

☆

*A treat for a hot day which is filling enough to serve instead of a meal.*

### INGREDIENTS

FOR 4

1 pt (600ml) strong black coffee

2 oz (50g) plain chocolate

8 scoops coffee ice cream

Make the coffee freshly and leave it to cool. Break the chocolate into small pieces and put into a basin over hot water. Heat until melted and then leave to cool.

Just before serving, put the coffee and chocolate into a blender and mix well. Add the ice cream and blend until thick and creamy. Pour into tall glasses and serve with straws.

## ICED CHOCOLATE

☆

*A refreshing but nourishing drink for a hot day.*
*The syrup may be prepared in advance and stored*
*in the refrigerator for a day or two.*

### INGREDIENTS
FOR 4–6
8 oz (225g) caster sugar
½ pt (300ml) water
2 oz (50g) cocoa powder
1 teasp coffee powder
2 pt (1.2l) chilled milk

Put the sugar and water into a heavy-based pan and heat gently until the sugar has dissolved. Bring to the boil, but do not stir, and boil for about 5 minutes to make a thin syrup. Remove from the heat and whisk in the cocoa powder and coffee powder until there are no lumps. Return to low heat and simmer for 3 minutes. Pour into a jug and chill in the refrigerator. Whisk in the chilled milk just before serving.

## CHOCOLATE LIÈGEOIS

☆

*The richest chocolate drink, which may be served at the*
*end of a meal instead of a pudding and coffee.*

### INGREDIENTS
FOR 4
¼ pt (150ml) Chocolate Syrup (p117)
1 pt (600ml) creamy milk
4 scoops chocolate or vanilla ice cream
¼ pt (150ml) double cream
2 teasp caster sugar
cocoa powder

Mix the Chocolate Syrup and milk until evenly coloured and pour into four tall chilled glasses. Add a scoop of ice cream to each glass. Whip the cream and sugar to stiff peaks and divide among the glasses. Sprinkle lightly with cocoa powder and serve at once with straws and long spoons.

*Chocolate Liègeois*

# 12

# FANCY BITS

..........................................

Since most chocolate dishes are very dark in colour, they can also appear flat and dull. Their appearance is greatly enhanced by the addition of smooth, shiny chocolate decorations which are easily prepared.

## Squares, Triangles and Other Shapes

Melt plain chocolate and spread thinly with a palette knife on a completely flat sheet of baking parchment. Leave to set at room temperature until firm but not brittle. Use a sharp knife to cut squares or triangles, or use cake or cocktail cutters for circles and other shapes. Lift carefully from the baking parchment. Any offcuts may be melted and used again.

## Leaves

Choose fresh leaves which are not poisonous and which have an attractive shape and prominent veining (rose leaves are ideal). Wash and dry the leaves thoroughly. Brush one surface of each leaf thickly and evenly with melted chocolate, preferably using the heavily veined side. Arrange on a sheet of baking parchment and leave until the chocolate is hard. Peel off the leaves carefully.

## Lace

Draw triangles or circles on baking parchment. Put melted chocolate into a small piping bag with a small writing pipe and pipe round the outline of each shape. Fill in with lacy lines. Leave to set at room temperature. Lift very carefully from the paper.

# Palm Trees

Use a small piping bag with a writing pipe, and fill with melted chocolate. Pipe a six-pointed starfish shape on to baking parchment. Pipe on a trunk from the centre, giving a ringed effect by using short horizontal lines. Leave to set at room temperature.

# Caraque (Long Curls)

Melt plain chocolate and spread with a palette knife less than $\frac{1}{4}$in (5mm) thick on clean dry marble or a laminated surface. Leave to set at room temperature. Using a long knife, hold the blade at an angle of 45° to the surface and push away from the body, shaving off long curls. Lift off carefully with a skewer or pointed knife. Small flakes which break off may also be used as decoration or may be melted and used again.

# Short Curls

Use a thick block of plain chocolate or cake covering, as French cooking chocolate is too hard and brittle for this technique. Use at room temperature, and scrape off curls of chocolate with a potato peeler (the type with a light, thin rotary blade is easiest to use). Do not handle the curls which melt easily, but lift them with the point of a knife directly on to the surface to be decorated.

# Grated Chocolate

Use a thick block of plain chocolate or cake covering and chill for 30 minutes in the refrigerator. Use the coarse side of the grater for preparing the chocolate.

# Chocolate Horns

Use cream-horn tins which have been washed and dried. Rub the insides with kitchen paper to make them shiny. Pour in melted chocolate and tilt the horn moulds so that the inside is evenly coated. Leave to set and then repeat the process to make a thicker casing which will be easier to unmould. Leave to set in a cool place and when the chocolate has set hard, ease out with the point of a knife. For small horns which are suitable for *petits fours*, paint the chocolate only a short way up the outside of the horn moulds. Leave to set and repeat the process. When the chocolate is hard, slip it out of the moulds.

# Cake and Sweet Bases

Put together paper or foil cake or sweet cases in pairs to provide a firm base. Paint chocolate thinly inside the inner case to cover completely. Leave until hard and then repeat the process. When the chocolate has set, peel off the outer cases and use the chocolate shapes for filling with liqueurs, truffle mixture, soft fruit, fondant, etc.

# LIST OF RECIPES

## Chocolate Classics

Chocolate Marquise 16

Marjolaine 17

Dobos Torte 19

Bûche de Noël 20

Devil's Food 20

Cassata 21

Sacher Torte 22

Black Forest Gâteau 22

Nègre en Chemise 23

Chocolate Eclairs 25

## Hot Puddings

Hot Chocolate Meringue Pudding 26

Chocolate Cream Pancakes 27

Chocolate Walnut Pudding 27

Saucy Mocha Pudding 28

Hot Chocolate Betty 28

Chocolate Apricot Crumble 29

Chocolate Fondue 29

Chocolate Eggy Bread 30

Rum Hazelnut Pudding 30

Chocolate Fudge Pudding 31

Chocolate Almond Pudding 31

Chocolate Upside-down Pudding 32

White Chocolate Pudding 32

Steamed Chocolate Soufflé 33

Little Chocolate Cream Soufflés 33

Hot Chocolate Soufflé 35

Helen's Pancake Layer 35

## Cold Puddings

Chocolate Rumpots 36

Double Chocolate Fudge Flan 37

Chocolate Mousse Cake 37

Chocolate Pavement 38

Little Chocolate Custards 38

Chocolate Fruit Brulée 39

Délice au Chocolat 39

Chilled Chocolate Soufflé 40

Chocolate Roulade 40

Chocolate Hazelnut Gâteau 42

Mocha Icebox Cake 42

Chocolate Chestnut Loaf 43

Chocolate Cream Sophie 43

Julia's Chocolate Dinner Cake 44

Wicked Chocolate Roll 44

Mocha Charlotte 45

Chocolate Syllabub 45

Devil's Mountain 46

Mocha Rum Creams 46

Profiteroles 47

Hungarian Mocha Gâteau 47

Chocolate Truffle 48

Fudge Pots 49

Chocolate Crackling Flan 49

White Chocolate Terrine 51

Chocolate Pavlova 51

Saint Emilion au Chocolate 52

Floating Islands in a Chocolate Sea 52

Baked Chocolate Cheesecake 53

Chilled Chocolate Cheesecake 53

Chocolate Zabaglione 54

Mont Blanc 54

Chocolate Chestnut Gâteau 55

Double Chocolate Mousse 55

Chocolate Mousse 56

Brandy Cream Mousse 56

Mars Bar Mousse 57

White Chocolate Mousse 57

## Ices

Rum Bumble Ice 59

Rum Parfait 59

Dark Chocolate Ice Cream 61

Chocolate Granita 61

White Chocolate Ice Cream 61

Chocolate Rum Sorbet 62

Double Chocolate Ice Cream 62

Chocolate Fudge Ice Cream 63

Brown Bread Chocolate Ice Cream 63

Frozen Chocolate Soufflé 64

Peppermint Cream Ice 64

Nutty Chocolate Terrine 65

Frozen Mocha Mousse 65

Coffee Truffle Bombe with Mocha Cream Sauce 67

Mocha Ice Cream 67

Chocolate Fruit Bombe 68

Chocolate Brandy Terrine 68

## Cakes and Biscuits

Chocolate Bran Cake 70

Chocolate Ginger Cake 70

Chocolate Caramel Cake 71

Chocolate Rum Cake 71

Chocolate Parkin 72

Chocolate Marble Cake 72

Rich Dark Chocolate Cake 74

Brazilian Chocolate Cake 74

Chocolate Fudge Layer Cake 75

Chocolate Teabread 75

Never-fail Chocolate Cake 76

Chocolate Chip Orange Cake 76

Austrian Chocolate Cake 77

Panforte 77

Chocolate Baba 78

Chocolate Whisky Cake 80

Chocolate Hazelnut Cake 80

Triple Cake 81

Truffle Roll 82

Chocolate Ginger Cup Cakes 82

Cup Cakes 83

Chocolate Fruit Celebration Cake 83

Sicilian Chocolate Squares 84

Truffle Cakes 84

Chocolate Meringues 85

Crunch Brownies 85

Syrup Brownies 86

Chocolate Fudge Squares 86

Chocolate Flapjacks 87

One-pot Brownies 87

Chocolate Macaroons 87

Picnic Bars 88

Chocolate Marshmallow Shortbread 88

No-bake Chocolate Squares 89

Turtles 89

Hungarian Mocha Cookies 90

Chocolate Chip Walnut Cookies 90

Hazelnut Crisps 91

Viennese Chocolate Shells 91

Chocolate Lemon Bourbons 92

Florentines 92

Chocolate Rings 93

Chocolate Chip Raisin Cookies 93

Chocolate Chip Shortbread 94

Chocolate Coconut Bars 94

White Chocolate Fruit Bars 95

Chocolate Maple Bars 95

Rum Raisin Toffee Bars 96

Peanut Brownies 96

Chocolate Croissants 97

## Sweetmeats and Petits Fours

Fresh Cream Truffles 99

Liqueur Truffles 99

Double Truffles 100

White Chocolate Truffles 100

Parisian Truffles 102

Walnut Truffles 102

Chocolate Orange Truffles 102

Rum and Almond Truffles 103

Rum Truffles 103

Rich Orange Truffles 103

Chocolate Fudge 104

Chocolate Cinnamon Fudge 104

Uncooked Chocolate Fudge 105

Chocolate Orange Creams 105

Praline Log 106

Chocolate Torrone 106

Chocolate Snaps 107

Colettes 107

Chocolate Almond Crunch 108

Chocolate Cherry Creams 108

Crazy Pavement 109

Chocolate Pralines 109

Chocolate Strawberries 109

Chocolate Crunchies 110

Chocolate Coconut Ice 110

Orange Thins 110

## Sauces

Chocolate Sauce 111

Mocha Cream Sauce 111

Chocolate Whipped Custard 112

Chocolate Mousseline Sauce 112

Mocha Sauce 112

Dark Chocolate Rum Sauce 113

Chocolate Butterscotch Sauce 113

Chocolate Mousse Sauce 113

Chocolate Fudge Sauce 114

Mint Cream 114

Coffee Custard Sauce 114

Mars Bar Sauce 114

Orange Sauce 115

Raspberry Liqueur Sauce 115

Crème Anglaise 115

## Drinks

Chocolate Nog 116

Basic Chocolate Syrup 117

Real Cocoa 117

Chocolate Toddy 117

Swiss Chocolate 118

Breakfast Chocolate 118

Mexican Chocolate 118

Chocolate Milk Shake 119

Chocolate Ice Cream Soda 119

Mocha Cooler 119

Iced Chocolate 120

Chocolate Liègeois 120

# INDEX

Almond
  Crunch, Chocolate 108
  Pudding, Chocolate 31
Apricot Crumble, Chocolate 29
Austrian Chocolate Cake 77

Baba, Chocolate 78
Bars
  Chocolate Coconut 94
  Chocolate Maple 95
  Picnic 88
  Rum Raisin Toffee 96
  White Chocolate Fruit 95
Betty, Hot Chocolate 28
Black Forest Gâteau 22
Bombe
  Chocolate Fruit 68
  with Mocha Cream Sauce,
    Coffee Truffle 67
Bourbons, Chocolate Lemon 92
Bran Cake, Chocolate 70
Brandy
  Cream Mousse 56
  Terrine, Chocolate 68
Brazilian Chocolate Cake 74
Bread, Chocolate Eggy 30
Breakfast Chocolate 118
Brown Bread Chocolate Ice
  Cream 63
Brownies
  Crunch 85
  One-pot 87
  Peanut 96
  Syrup 86
Bûche de Noël 20

Cake
  Austrian Chocolate 77
  Brazilian Chocolate 74
  Chocolate Bran 70
  Chocolate Caramel 71
  Chocolate Chip Orange 76
  Chocolate Fruit Celebration
    83

Chocolate Fudge Layer 75
Chocolate Ginger 70
Chocolate Hazelnut 80
Chocolate Marble 72
Chocolate Rum 71
Chocolate Whisky 80
Mocha Icebox 42
Never-fail Chocolate 76
Rich Dark Chocolate 74
Triple 81
Cakes, Truffle 84
caramel 13
Caramel Cake, Chocolate 71
Cassata 21
Charlotte, Mocha 45
Cheesecake
  Baked Chocolate 53
  Chilled Chocolate 53
Cherry Creams, Chocolate 108
Chestnut
  Gâteau, Chocolate 55
  Loaf, Chocolate 43
chocolate
  bitter 7
  chips 8
  melting 10–11
  milk 8
  plain 7
  storage 10
  white 8
cocoa powder 8, 12
Cocoa, Real 117
Coconut
  Bars, Chocolate 94
  Ice, Chocolate 110
coffee 14
Coffee Truffle Bombe with
  Mocha Cream Sauce 67
Colettes 107
Cookies
  Chocolate Chip Raisin 93
  Chocolate Chip Walnut 90
  Hungarian Mocha 90
cooking chocolate 8

couverture 8
Crazy Pavement 109
Cream Sophie, Chocolate 43
Creams, Mocha Rum 46
Crème Anglaise 115
Crisps, Hazelnut 91
Croissants, Chocolate 97
Crumble, Chocolate Apricot 29
Crunch Brownies 85
Crunch, Chocolate Almond
  108
Crunchies, Chocolate 110
Cup Cakes 83; Chocolate
  Ginger 82
Custard, Chocolate Whipped
  112
Custards, Little Chocolate 38

Dark Chocolate Ice Cream 61
Délice au Chocolat 39
Devil's Food 20
Devil's Mountain 46
Dinner Cake, Julia's Chocolate 44
Dobos Torte 19
Double Chocolate
  Ice Cream 62
  Mousse 55
drinking chocolate powder 10

Eclairs, Chocolate 25
Eggy Bread, Chocolate 30

Flan
  Chocolate Crackling 49
  Double Chocolate Fudge 37
Flapjacks, Chocolate 87
Floating Islands in a Chocolate
  Sea 52
Florentines 92
Fondue, Chocolate 29
Frozen Mocha Mousse 65
Fruit
  Bars, White Chocolate 95
  Bombe, Chocolate 68

Brulée, Chocolate 39
Celebration Cake, Chocolate
  83
fruit 14; dried 13
Fudge
  Chocolate 104
  Chocolate Cinnamon 104
  Ice Cream, Chocolate 63
  Layer Cake, Chocolate 75
  Pots 49
  Pudding, Chocolate 31
  Squares, Chocolate 86
  Uncooked Chocolate 105

Gâteau
  Black Forest 22
  Chocolate Chestnut 55
  Chocolate Hazelnut 42
  Hungarian Mocha 47
Ginger
  Cake, Chocolate 70
  Cup Cakes, Chocolate 82
Granita, Chocolate 61

Hazelnut
  Cake, Chocolate 80
  Crisps 91
  Gâteau, Chocolate 42
Helen's Pancake Layer 35
herbs 14
Hot Chocolate Soufflé 35
Hungarian Mocha
  Cookies 90
  Gâteau 47

Ice
  Chocolate Coconut 110
  Rum Bumble 59
Ice Cream
  Brown Bread Chocolate 63
  Chocolate Fudge 63
  Dark Chocolate 61
  Double Chocolate 62
  Mocha 67

Soda, Chocolate 119
White Chocolate 61
Icebox Cake, Mocha 42
Iced Chocolate 120

Julia's Chocolate Dinner Cake 44

Lemon Bourbons, Chocolate 92
Liègeois, Chocolate 120
liqueurs 14
Little Chocolate Custards 38
Loaf, Chocolate Chestnut 43

Macaroons, Chocolate 87
Maple Bars, Chocolate 95
Marble Cake, Chocolate 72
Marjolaine 17
Marquise, Chocolate 16
Mars Bar Mousse 57
Marshmallow Shortbread,
    Chocolate 88
Meringue Pudding, Hot
    Chocolate 26
Meringues, Chocolate 85
Mexican Chocolate 118
Milk Shake, Chocolate 119
Mint Cream 114
Mocha
    Charlotte 45
    Cooler 119
    Ice Cream 67
    Icebox Cake 42
    Rum Creams 46
Mont Blanc 54
Mousse
    Brandy Cream 56
    Cake, Chocolate 37
    Chocolate 56
    Double Chocolate 55
    Frozen Mocha 65
    Mars Bar 57
    White Chocolate 57

Nègre en Chemise 23
Never-fail Chocolate Cake 76

No-bake Chocolate Squares
    89
Nog, Chocolate 116
nuts 13
Nutty Chocolate Terrine 65

Orange
    Cake, Chocolate Chip 76
    Creams, Chocolate 105
    Thins 110

Pancake Layer, Helen's 35
Pancakes, Chocolate Cream 27
Panforte 77
Parfait, Rum 59
Parkin, Chocolate 72
Pavement, Chocolate 38
Pavlova, Chocolate 51
Peanut Brownies 96
Peppermint Cream Ice 64
Picnic Bars 88
Praline Log 106
Pralines, Chocolate 109
Profiteroles 47
Pudding
    Chocolate Almond 31
    Chocolate Fudge 31
    Chocolate Upside-down 32
    Chocolate Walnut 27
    Hot Chocolate Meringue 26
    Rum Hazelnut 30
    Saucy Mocha 28
    White Chocolate 32

Raisin Cookies, Chocolate Chip
    93
Rich Dark Chocolate Cake 74
Rings, Chocolate 93
Roll
    Truffle 82
    Wicked Chocolate 44
Roulade, Chocolate 40
Rum
    Bumble Ice 59
    Cake, Chocolate 71

Hazelnut Pudding 30
Parfait 59
Raisin Toffee Bars 96
Sorbet, Chocolate 62
Rumpots, Chocolate 36

Sacher Torte 22
Saint Emilion au Chocolate 52
Sauce
    Chocolate 111
    Chocolate Butterscotch 113
    Chocolate Fudge 114
    Chocolate Mousse 113
    Chocolate Mousseline 112
    Coffee Custard 114
    Dark Chocolate Rum 113
    Mars Bar 114
    Mocha Cream 111
    Orange 115
    Raspberry Liqueur 115
Saucy Mocha Pudding 28
Shells, Viennese Chocolate 91
Shortbread
    Chocolate Chip 94
    Chocolate Marshmallow 88
Sicilian Chocolate Squares 84
Snaps, Chocolate 107
Sophie, Chocolate Cream 43
Sorbet, Chocolate Rum 62
Soufflé
    Chilled Chocolate 40
    Frozen Chocolate 64
    Hot Chocolate 35
    Steamed Chocolate 33
Soufflés, Little Chocolate
    Cream 33
spices 14
Squares
    No-bake Chocolate 89
    Sicilian Chocolate 84
Strawberries, Chocolate 109
Swiss Chocolate 118
Syllabub, Chocolate 45
Syrup, Basic Chocolate 117
Syrup Brownies 86

Teabread, Chocolate 75
Terrine
    Chocolate Brandy 68
    Nutty Chocolate 65
    White Chocolate 51
Toddy, Chocolate 117
Torrone, Chocolate 106
Triple Cake 81
Truffle
    Cakes 84
    Chocolate 48
    Roll 82
Truffles
    Chocolate Orange 102
    Double 100
    Fresh Cream 99
    Liqueur 99
    Parisian 102
    Rich Orange 103
    Rum 103
    Rum and Almond 103
    Walnut 102
    White Chocolate 100
Turtles 89

Upside-down Pudding,
    Chocolate 32

Viennese Chocolate Shells 91

Walnut
    Cookies, Chocolate Chip 90
    Pudding, Chocolate 27
Whisky Cake, Chocolate 80
White Chocolate
    Fruit Bars 95
    Ice Cream 61
    Mousse 57
    Pudding 32
    Terrine 51
    Truffles 100
Wicked Chocolate Roll 44
wine 15

Zabaglione, Chocolate 54